D0053104

Love Magic

Lexa Roséan ☆

Also by Laurie Cabot:

and Tom Cowan

POWER OF THE WITCH:
THE EARTH, THE MOON, AND
THE MAGICAL PATH TO ENLIGHTENMENT

and Jean Mills

CELEBRATE THE EARTH:
A YEAR OF HOLIDAYS IN
THE PAGAN TRADITION

Love Magic

Laurie Cabot

with

Tom Cowan

Delta
Trade Paperbacks

A DELTA BOOK
Published by
Dell Publishing
a division of
Bantam Doubleday Dell Publishing Group, Inc.
1540 Broadway
New York, New York 10036

Copyright © 1992 by Laurie Cabot and Tom Cowan

All rights reserved. No part of this book may be
reproduced or transmitted in any form or by any means,
electronic or mechanical, including photocopying, recording,
or by any information storage and retrieval system,
without the written permission of the
Publisher, except where permitted by law.

The trademark Delta® is registered
in the U.S. Patent and Trademark Office and in other countries.

Library of Congress Cataloging in Publication Data

Cabot, Laurie.
    Love magic / Laurie Cabot and Tom Cowan.
      p.   cm.
    ISBN 0-385-30570-2
    1. Magic.   2. Love—Miscellanea.   I. Cowan, Tom,
1944–   II. Title.
BF1623.L6C33   1992
133.4'42—dc20   91-37418   CIP

Book design by Christine Swirnoff

Manufactured in the United States of America

Published simultaneously in Canada

June 1992

10 9 8 7 6 5

BVG

To our parents

Acknowledgments

Many kind and dedicated people encouraged us and supported our efforts in writing this book. Among them are our editors, Jody Rein and Catherine Chapman, our agent, Susan Lee Cohen, and special friends and associates like Kate Arment, Nancy St. Lawrence, Joan Gormalley, Marie Cardillo, and Karen Thorn.

Contents

Introduction

O<small>N A VISIT</small> to England, the home of my ancestors, I fell in love with a country gentleman. I wasn't sure just how much he cared for me, even though we spent long hours and even days together, driving through the English countryside, having tea at romantic rustic inns, and staying up late to watch the stars. One afternoon while I was alone, doubts began to cross my mind. Does he really love me the way I love him? I would find out.

I hiked out into the hills beyond Stratford-upon-Avon dragging my Witch's sword behind me. With it, I carved a circle into the earth near the ancient standing stones called "The Roll Rite" and lifted my voice to invoke the powers of that magical land. "If he loves me as I love him, bring the mist of the dragon and lead him to me now!" As I walked back a mist began to form, and when I arrived at the manor house where I was staying, my English lover was just driving in the gate. He rolled down the window of his antique car and said, "All of a sudden I had this burning desire to see you!"

Love Magic is a book of Witches' spells and rituals to attract love and enhance relationships. You do not need to be a Witch or even be in love with a Witch to use this book. In fact, *Love Magic* is written both as a sensible guide for readers who already practice magic and as an introduction for people who know nothing about it. I hope that adepts of the magical arts as well as novices will find the book useful, entertaining, and enlightening.

From our own separate backgrounds Tom and I weave together several rich traditions and many years of experience.

I am an ordained High Priestess of Witchcraft, descended from Celtic ancestry with Faerie blood coursing through my veins. Love magic has always been a vital ingredient in my life as it is in any Witch's daily practices because there is little that is more important than warmth, caring, affection, and pleasure. I first began my study and practice of Witchcraft forty-two years ago, when practitioners were virtually nonexistent. Knowledge of the Craft was closely guarded and, because of the fear of persecution, confined to family traditions. The lack of information about real magic created within me a passionate determination to uncover the reality of Witchcraft and master the Art.

Since that time, I have founded the Cabot Tradition of the Science of Witchcraft, which blends scientific and natural law with psychic abilities and Witchcraft practices. I have shared my knowledge of ancient and modern Celtic Witchcraft, the Egyptian Mysteries, Hermetics, Spellcraft, Herbcraft, psychic healing, ritual magic, and mental alchemy with thousands of people who have attended my classes and seminars over the past thirty-three years. I have also organized and led public rituals as well officiated at sacred functions in Salem. It has been a joy and confirmation of my efforts to see the explosive growth of the modern Craft. Indeed, Witches are now once again members of an international and ageless community that preserves ancient wisdom and worships the Great Mother, She who was old when the world was young.

Tom has been a student and teacher of shamanic practices and other visionary work for twenty years. His work has roots in "core shamanism" as well as in specific strains of Native American spirituality and the Celtic origins of modern Witchcraft. As a North American and the son of families going back to Celtic and Germanic ancestors, he unites the Old Ways of both places in his personal spiritual life. Tom has helped organize public rituals in New York City to celebrate pagan earth holidays. He is active in the grass-roots dreamwork movement and the neo-pagan revival to reintroduce the ancient folk customs to modern Americans. He lectures extensively on dreams, shamanism, and mysticism.

Our understanding of magic webs backward into the very distant past and forward into what we hope to create for the twenty-first century, while our understanding of love and human relationships derives from the people we have loved in our own lives and from the joys, hopes, and sorrows brought to us by the people we advise as spiritual counselors.

No one has all the answers or insights, or even knows all the questions, about a subject as profound and mysterious as the human heart. It is therefore with utmost respect for my readers, who may see more keenly into the mysteries of love than I do, that I offer whatever knowledge and experience the Goddess and God have given to me.

I encourage those of you already experienced with magic to use the spells and rituals as springboards for creating your own work. The most powerful spells always come from the heart and mind of the magic-worker, not from the pages of a book. For readers new to magic, I suggest you peruse the entire book before attempting any spells and rituals, then begin with the ones that seem most appropriate for your own needs and your own level of spiritual practice.

The book is divided into three parts. The first (Chapters 1 to 3) presents an overview of magic and love. The second part (Chapters 4 to 6) contains rituals and meditations for self-discovery and self-esteem, both necessary for magic and love. The last section contains three chapters of specific spells and rituals for attracting a lover, for enhancing a relationship, and for ending a relationship. The final chapter shows how to find the ingredients for love magic in the natural environment.

To use this book, you don't have to change your religious or metaphysical beliefs to work spells and rituals. In some cases, you may have to "suspend disbelief" about magic, much like you suspend your knowledge at the theater that the action of the play is only "acting." In most cases, you don't have to *believe* anything specific. But, as in all areas of life, it is necessary to have a strong and abiding belief in yourself and the greater Power that creates and fills the cosmos.

Magic is a craft, a set of practices, a way of focusing your will and intention. It is something you do, not something you believe and it works remarkably well for people of widely varying belief systems.

Some readers may ask: What is a Witch? How does a person become one? I refer you to our first book *Power of the Witch,* where I deal with these questions more thoroughly. But to satisfy your curiosity, I can say briefly: Witchcraft is rooted in the pre-Christian spiritual and healing practices of the early European cultures. Like ancient people everywhere, the first Witches were earth-oriented people, in love with the changing Wheel of Life manifested in the seasons of the year, the animal and plant life with which they shared the planet, and the powers of the mind and heart. They found the earth to be wondrously alive with spirits and deities, with elemental powers charged with divine energy, and with marvelous opportunities to dream and wonder about human life: its origins, its purpose, its destiny. They found answers and intimations of answers to their dreams and questions in the natural world around them and in their relationships with each other. Witches are people who strive to keep alive these ancient visions of the natural harmony and balance of nature and to participate in the Wheel of Life.

And how does a person become a Witch? How do you know you are not a Witch already?

Love Magic

THE YOUNG CELTIC God Aengus Og met a dream-woman from the Land of Faerie, and fell in love with her at once. For a year she appeared to him in dreams, playing a magical stringed instrument that lulled him into the deepest sleep. Longing to be with this Faerie woman by day, he grew lovesick, never knowing where she went at dawn. He lost all interest in food and life. Eventually, Aengus learned that his Faerie lover spent every other year in the form of a white swan on a certain lake with 150 other swans. On October 31, the Holy Day of Samhain, the Witches' New Year, when the veil between this world and the world of Faerie is lifted, Aengus went to the lake and saw the swans. He called to his beloved and promised to stay with her. She came to him, and immediately the magic of this union turned the young God into a beautiful swan. That night, after more than a year of desperate longing, Aengus slept with the woman of his dreams and fulfilled his heart's desire. Later the two swans flew back to Aengus's home, singing enchanted love songs that caused all who heard them to sleep and dream for three blissful days.

The story of Aengus Og happens every day. In our deepest, heartfelt moments, we fall in love, grow lovesick, can't eat, dream of our heart's desire, discover that love radically transforms us and that our happiness spills over into the lives of others. In short, falling in love is magical, and love itself is a form of magic that transforms and excites not just the lovers but those around them.

I watch seekers of love and magic search through our Witch shop in Salem, and I know that magical bookstores across the nation are filled with people looking for just the right herb, crystal, charm, or book of spells to bring them true love. Some are successful in their quest; others are not. Magic, it is true, can bring about change in the flash of an eye, but it is no substitute for the personal growth and transformation required to make a loving relationship prosper. A spell or charm may bring you a new love, and magic rituals may help two lovers get off to a good start or get back on track, but only personal commitment makes a relationship last. Magic-workers have to work hard at love just like everyone else, and even more importantly, work on themselves. We are physical beings and must bring our magic down to earth and work with it every day.

Magic is the ability to alter one's state of consciousness at will in order to effect some change in the world and Witches use many different techniques to achieve this. Salem Witches use simple, nonthreatening methods to shift our consciousness gently into an alpha wave state. We believe that whatever we change by magical means must be for the good of all and that it harm no one. We follow strictly the ancient law of Witchcraft that our actions—both good and bad—will return to us three-fold.

What happens in an altered state of consciousness? Alpha is a springboard to magic, but it is only the first step. To excel at magic, work is required. You have to *do* something. Most spells involve action utilizing magical tools and psychic stimuli to catalyze the spell. Sometimes it's possible to do magic with the mind alone, but material objects contain their own energy and thus activities done with those objects help strengthen concentration and provide a focal point for our attention.

Thoughts are energy. The mind is energy. The latest scientific reports indicate that mental energy is electrochemical in nature. Scientists confess, however, that for all their progress in understanding the brain, mental energy is still elusive and mysterious. How does one explain in a rational manner, for example, the many occurrences in parapsychology: precognition, extrasensory perception, telepathy, psychokinesis? Clearly some type of mental energy is involved with these phenomena, but it sometimes seems to have "a mind of its own," so to speak. It leaps and darts where it will, bringing information to individuals outside the customary channels of perception, and in so doing, it disrupts the rational, fact-based paradigm the modern world uses to explain how the universe operates. Witches who practice our science, however, know that this energy can be controlled.

We believe the energy of the mind is the same energy that charges the entire universe. We all live in fields of common consciousness, much like fish swimming in a common sea. And like fish, we are able to stir the waters, send out ripples, and generate currents in all directions. When specific flows of energy intersect, energy exchanges occur between the objects generating those currents. To conceptualize this in another way, it may help to think of the universe as a giant web, on which each person, animal, plant, and object holds a thread of energy connected to every other thread. Or imagine each individual with a personal radar transmitter beaming a frequency of light outward in all directions and the beams intersecting with the beamed frequencies from other creatures. By placing our attention upon the web lines or the light lines, we can direct and guide energy to any other entity.

Sometimes at night you will see two searchlights scanning the sky, swinging their beams in great arcs across the heavens. Their lights cross for a moment, and the two become one at the point of intersection, and the intensity of light increases. Mental energy directed outward during a spell or ritual operates in the same way. When doing magic, you send your energy, your thoughts, outward, directed toward some person, object, or situation, increasing the energy at that point to cause a desired change.

The experience of "love at first sight" illustrates how a magical chemistry can influence two people spontaneously without any conscious effort to do so. Two individuals see each other for the first time, their eyes meet, and two "beams" of energy intersect. Something clicks. Information is exchanged. In that magical moment, both of them know that "this could be the start of something."

SYMBOLS AND IMAGES

A symbol is an image enriched with thought and feeling. It has meaning. Symbols embody concepts and associations that can be personal and private as well as universal and shared with others. In a magical sense, symbols and images are the nodes where currents of consciousness intersect. A symbol channels magic. Some symbols are activated by the work of the person doing magic; others are so powerful they influence us regardless of whether anyone is using them for magical purposes. The nation's flag, for example, does not have to be "activated" to generate feelings of patriotism. Over many years it has received the energy of millions of Americans, and it is now fully charged. A dozen roses are a symbol of love. Generations of lovers have fully charged them and their meaning is now obvious.

In the Western world, various symbologies have emerged as potent channels for magical work, precisely because so many people have put their energy into them and activated them over such a long period of time: the signs of the Zodiac, the Tarot, the Kabbala, the Runic alphabet of northern Europe, the tools of alchemy, the major pantheons of Gods and Goddesses, and the many wonderful legends and folklore arising from the deep mythic reservoirs of Western consciousness. Each generation infuses these symbols and images with its own psychic energy and, in the process, reinforces the genetic memory of these symbols for future generations.

Anyone serious about doing magic will construct a pattern of symbols, legends, myths, and images with which to work. While it might be said that any symbol and image will work, not every symbol or image will work for everyone. We each have our preferences. Some images come from our personal unconscious: dreams, old memories, and fantasies residing just below our conscious field of awareness. These exert powerful influences on our conscious thoughts and feelings, even though we are not always aware of them, but rituals and meditations do help bring these images out.

Other symbols arise from archetypal images shared by human beings the world over by virtue of our common humanity.

These images resonate with strangely similar meanings and powers in whatever century or culture they appear. The young hero, the wise elder, the beautiful lover, the dark journey at night, the deep cave or sea, the blessed dawn, the intelligent animal companion, the beast or foe, the hidden treasure, the weapons of strength and power—all cultures have their variations of these images, and on the right occasions they become activated in forms appropriate to the culture in which we live. A successful spell or ritual will summon these images. At such times, we feel we are in the presence of a Goddess or Spirit, some grand force or energy moving through us, helping to empower our magic.

For our spells and rituals I have chosen many symbols and images from our Celtic heritage because Tom and I believe they have the power to work for most individuals in Western culture. The major images of Celtic folklore constitute a symbology of their own: the princess imprisoned in a castle, the Witch Queen stirring her potion, a Faerie Goddess granting wishes on a golden ring, the magical tools of chalice, sword, and harp, not to mention all the symbols and images associated with the Merlin and Arthur traditions. We realize not every symbol will work for every reader. Some of the symbols come from very ancient practices that appeal to the two of us for personal reasons and that we use in our own personal magic. As in dreams, everyone produces symbols with personal meaning and significance. Some people always dream about rivers or high buildings or their parents. Others never dream about these things; they have their own dream images.

No particular set of deities, tools, or settings is absolutely crucial for a given spell, although I believe the ones I suggest are the most magical. If you are already experienced in doing ritual and working magic, you may want to use our structures and add your own symbolic content. What is important is that the symbols work for you. If a particular spell or ritual involves symbols and images alien to your views, change it. Substitute similar ones that retain the spirit of the ritual but are more compatible with your own frame of reference. As you read through the spells and rituals in this book, notice your reaction to the symbols and images I suggest. They should give you feelings of power and excitement. If they do not resonate favorably with you, skip the spell, or change the symbols. If you're a novice to this work, you should probably do the spells and rituals as I describe them and change them later as you become more experienced.

Ritual is a more or less formalized use of symbols and may be either public or private. You can use symbols without ritual. Any symbol, for example, can be used mentally, just by its being thought of and held in one's awareness. But it assumes greater power in an external form, and it can produce even more power in the kind of dramatic activity called ritual because dramatic activity generates energy of itself. An example: A common symbol in the Craft is the pentacle. Meditating on its significance empowers and inspires us. The star represents our highest aspirations. Common expressions such as "Reach for a star," "Hitch your wagon to a star," and "When you wish upon a star" attest to the universal significance of stars as symbols. The five points of the star can stand for the five extremities of the human body (head, hands, and feet) or the five senses through which we experience and appreciate the physical world represented by the circle around it. The circle, too, is an ancient universal symbol of wholeness, the God and Goddess, eternity, that which has no beginning or end. The star-within-the-circle is a rich symbol, a circuit channeling protection and universal wisdom. All it takes is a little mental energy playing with this symbol to release its power.

By giving the symbol a physical manifestation, however, a new dimension is added. Wearing a gold or silver pentacle, placing one in the center of an altar, or hanging it on a wall bring the pentacle's power right into the physical environment. It is more immediate. It has greater charge. Actively working with the pentacle in some physically dramatic way, as in a ritual, generates even more power. In Craft circles we trace a pentacle in the air with our athame (ritual knife) or wand. We might stand with our legs apart and arms raised outward at shoulder height to assume the pose of a five-pointed star. Often I like to trace a pentacle in the sand at the seashore and let the waves carry it out to sea. In whatever way we use the pentacle or its shape, we enhance its power and the power that it releases in us. The same is true for all symbols.

I encourage all my students to complement action performed in sacred space with a parallel action performed in the ordinary realm. Magic alone might achieve the goal, but ordinary, everyday efforts help, especially in matters of love. A ritual to attract a lover, or nurture your relationship, or save a relationship requires a corresponding activity in the ordinary world. There are many commonsense strategies that might help improve a relationship. Losing weight, fixing your hair, toning up your body, dressing attractively, acquiring hobbies and interests, learning about your partner's hobbies and interests, going out to meet people socially, taking courses to become more knowledgeable, reading books on self-improvement, joining clubs and organizations—these changes can help make you feel vital, attractive, interesting, and desirable. They will not guarantee love, of course, any more than will a love potion. But they increase your chances for meeting someone, attracting his or her interest, while at the same time increasing your self-esteem and giving you the personal and social skills to make a relationship work.

It is vitally important, therefore, to complement your magical workings with activities in the ordinary worlds of work, play, and home life. I know a Witch who didn't think he needed to rewrite his resumé, apply for jobs, and do well on interviews when he wanted to change careers to make more money. He thought it was enough just to just sit at home, draw the curtain, and burn prosperity incense in his cauldron! He tried magic alone and nothing happened. Then he performed rituals and spells to empower him to apply for jobs and to have confidence on interviews. He eventually found the right job. In his case, magic gave him the courage to pound the pavement.

THE PERILS OF FANTASY AND MANIPULATION

Two perils threaten the quest for love: fantasy and manipulation. A word about each.

Spells involve visualizing, which to the uninitiated can look a lot like mere fantasizing. There is a real danger here because being in love, or wishing you were in love, spontaneously generates reveries. How easy to daydream about love and sex, and indulge ourselves in fantasies. We don't want to discourage fantasies and reveries. But they are not the kind of visualization used in love spells.

One autumn at a pagan camp-out, Tom met a young Witch who complained to him that she was using one of my love potions but it was only attracting "trolls," as she put it. He asked her how she used it, and she replied that she "dabbed a little on" when she went out. She was having romantic fantasies about "the man of her dreams" but he just wasn't appearing. Tom suggested that instead she visualize herself with a compatible partner, someone with whom she had some emotional, intellectual, and physical rapport. That very weekend she met a male Witch, fell in love, and they were still together at the spring camp the following year!

What is the difference between fantasizing and visualizing? Spells require the *conscious* creation of images and the *projection* of them outward, into the world. Reverie, fantasy, and daydreams draw us inward and cut off awareness of the outside world. Projections, spells, and rituals do just the opposite.

Witches project their desired end results outward, where they will do some good. If a Witch sits and broods over a lost love or daydreams about how wonderful it would be to meet the right person, nothing will happen. She is holding the spell within. But when a Witch takes those same thoughts, processes them creatively within a ritual constructed of appropriate symbols, tools, and activities, and then releases her desires into the cosmos, magic happens. Witches conclude their spells with the phrase "So mote it be," to signify they are letting their magic go —and it is done!

Manipulating another person by means of a spell sparks serious discussion among responsible Witches concerned about the ethical use of power. There has been so much anti-Witch propaganda over the centuries centering around the image of the "evil" Witch who hexes and causes harm, that modern Witches take very seriously their responsibility to use their power for the good of all and to harm no one. Central to these discussions that appear in pagan publications and symposiums is the issue of manipulation. To what extent do spells manipulate others? Is it ethical to manipulate another human being, even for that person's own good? Can we ever really know what is in the best interests of another? Is it even possible to manipulate or control another against that person's wishes? There are no easy answers to these questions, and each can evoke different answers depending on the context in which it is asked.

If a spell or potion is created with the intention that it be "for the good of all" and "to harm no one," then it will not be an unethical use of power. I recall a love potion that "made the rounds," so to speak, and still managed to be for the good of all. It happened that some years ago April, a Witch friend, made a love potion for me just before I left for a vacation in Ireland. I thanked her but said the purpose of the trip was not love, so I would probably not use it. When I arrived, Brittany, my hostess, confided that she had lost sexual interest in her husband after their baby was born. She asked me if I had a love potion that might help her. I poured some of April's sweet-smelling oil in a small bottle and did a quick spell over it to transfer its power to Brittany and to ensure that the results be "for the good of all and to harm no one." Then I gave it to her.

Brittany began wearing it and, true to the spell, she became romantically interested in her husband that very night. But then a strange event occurred. Brittany's brother, Iain, suddenly broke up with a woman he had been going with for about two years (it had been a stormy relationship) and started flirting with me. We were extremely attracted to each other and went out a few times while I was staying in a cottage nearby. Our romance got serious enough that we began talking about the possibility of one or the other of us moving across the ocean to be together. Was this a new love? Why did it happen so suddenly? Later, Brittany told me that she hoped I wouldn't mind but after using the potion for herself, she put a few drops on her brother. Magically, the potion worked, and the spell enveloped me in a new romance. The original spell was done for the good

of all, and even though I added to the potion a spell for Brittany, and she passed a few drops of the oil onto Iain, it continued to be for the good of all, and it harmed no one. Neither Iain
nor I, by the way, sold our homes and moved, but we still
communicate and are loving friends. The woman whom Iain
left soon found another man and began a calmer and happier
relationship.

The issue of manipulation, like the act itself, is tricky. It
takes on added importance in the context of love magic because
love, even without magic spells, always involves some element
of manipulation. Why do you wear provocative perfume or cologne? Why spend so much money on your date? Why go to
the trouble of preparing a romantic dinner? Why do you wear
sexy clothes? The reasons are obvious: You want to influence
someone; you are indirectly trying to manipulate another's
thoughts and feelings by creating a powerful and attractive image of yourself at your best.

The art of seduction is found in all cultures. Today the
conventional symbols and rituals to win someone's heart include such things as a dozen roses, a heart-shaped box of
candy, candle-lit dinners for two, moonlight walks in a garden
or along a beach, lying in the grass on a warm spring day and
weaving necklaces out of wild clover, love letters, long and
intimate phone calls late at night. Every culture has its variations on these ways of wooing and winning the heart of an
intended lover. In general, no one would claim these innocent
forms of seduction or manipulation are wrong. In one sense,
this is what romance is all about, and it's fun.

In earlier, less self-questioning times, people believed that
"all's fair in love and war" but today we would not accept such
an innocent and naive posture.

Seduction is a two-edged sword: one is for lust, the other

for love. Ideally, swordplay between lovers is a mock battle with both parties enjoying the game, parrying their attacks and counterattacks with a certain amount of tongue-in-cheek exuberance. All's fair in this "war of love" because it is a game with mutually agreed upon rules. The stakes might be love or sex, or both, but the two lovers know where they are headed. When the friendly persuasion becomes less than friendly, and the swordplay becomes force, I believe that one or the other of the partners is no longer playing the game of seduction but is out for rape. At this point, manipulation becomes totally unethical.

Can a love spell be a form of psychic rape? If so, how do we prevent it?

Spells are a means of positioning and negotiating, the same friendly persuasion found in the gentle art of seduction, but on the psychic level. Through spells, lovers meet in "psychic trysts" to encourage each other to respond favorably on the physical level. Spells are never performed in a spirit of force, or to weaken another's free will.

Remember that magic is the ability to alter consciousness at will; or, put another way, it is the ability to direct mental energy by means of symbols to achieve some desired end. A spell avoids becoming psychic rape because it merely sends out one's desires and positions them in the psychic field around the lover, at which point (either consciously or unconsciously) he or she becomes aware of those desires, and responds or does not respond. A spell never strips another of free will. Any misguided attempt to do so is black magic and severely condemned under the Laws of the Craft. Furthermore, baneful magic actually weakens the strength of the spell. Why? Because the God and Goddess of the Universe are Love. You cannot work with their energy with the intention of perverting it against the very Law of Love, which is the union of two people *for the good of the other.* By performing the spell in the spirit that it be for the good of all, and the more convincing and honest you are about this, you have a greater chance for success, simply because you align your intentions with love itself.

Energy work always takes place within a greater energy flow. I do not control the Great Flow. I can guide, deflect, and direct it into channels, provided these channels do not attempt to go against its very nature. In addition, I always acknowledge and respect the natural laws, using them, working with them, flowing with them. Neither I nor anyone can ever change them.

The issue of compatibility is a good example of this in terms of love magic. No one's magic is powerful enough to make two naturally incompatible people compatible. You might be able to achieve a few weeks or months of happiness and fun, but two basically incompatible natures will not be able to sustain a long-term relationship. (This is not the same as bringing together opposites, which can and do attract.)

Spells are powerful, but do not be afraid to use your power, any more than you would hesitate to use your natural skills to plan a romantic dinner or vacation, or buy just the right kind of gift for a loved one. The power of the Witch is always power from within coming from self-knowledge, self-confidence, and self-esteem. It is never power over another. It is never the psychic equivalent of using physical power to intimidate, frighten, shame, or sexually force yourself upon someone. When working for the good of all, as you must do to abide by the ethical code of Witchcraft, you cannot do a spell to threaten or terrorize someone into succumbing to your desires. Love simply does not work that way. Your spell will not work.

I always teach my students in the Craft that workers of magic must exercise great discretion and discernment, examining their motives and repeatedly consecrating their magical workings to the good of all. Responsible Witches remind themselves daily that their powers are to harm no one.

Means and Ends

In casting a spell, I always visualize and project the desired *outcome,* not the means to that outcome. The logic is simple: While we may know what we want (and sometimes even this is iffy!), we don't usually know the best way to get it. From time to time we catch ourselves going about something in the wrong way, choosing inappropriate or even counterproductive means. The same is true in magic. There is always another way to do everything, and we must honestly admit that we don't always know the best way, or even another way.

But in magic, this is not a cause for worry. Magic calls upon the Great Intelligence behind the universe to work out the details. Our human role is to create the outcome in a rich and powerful thought-form or projection. Every projection has both the energy we put into it, plus the energy it attracts. Remember that the flow of energy is like a web or radar beam—somewhere out there our intentions intersect with the energy that will provide the best means for achieving them. The Goddess and God know best and will provide.

Your Head and Your Heart

Witches are sensitive. What I do always comes from my heart, and in matters of love I try not to forget my head. Magic requires both head and heart. It is not all mental activity; it involves feelings too. Put your head and your heart into your magic, and you empower your spell and yourself. But magic never requires becoming mentally obsessed or preoccupied, nor does it require excessive emoting. Thoughts and feelings are the real generators of psychic energy. You do not have to work them overtime. Like any energy source, they can burn out, run dry, go dead. When they do, you need time and space to regenerate. Do magic in moderation. Visualize and project your goals mentally, without becoming obsessed with them to the point that you can't get your mind off them. They should not turn into daydreams and feelings that monopolize your time and interfere with your work.

Magical Workings

FOUR basic skills are needed for doing the love spells and rituals in this book. They are: entering an alpha state of consciousness, casting a circle, charging tools and materials, and shapeshifting. Many of the spells require some combination of these practices. In the interest of space, I have not repeated the following instructions at the start of each spell, but I encourage you to get in the habit of beginning each spell, meditation, or ritual with these routines: Put yourself into an alpha state, cast a circle around the area in which you are going to work, charge whatever tools or objects you plan to use, and, when necessary, shapeshift your own consciousness into other objects. Then you are ready to begin your magical work. These skills are the heart of Craft magic, so practice them often until they become second nature to you. Remember that magic is the ability to change consciousness at will to effect some change in the external or internal worlds. The difference between powerful magic and mere wishful thinking often depends on how skillfully you can alter your consciousness by performing these basic techniques.

Alpha

There are various methods of changing brain activity from the normal beta waves associated with alert, wakeful consciousness to the deeper alpha waves typical of. visionary experience. While the methods vary among magicians, psychics, shamans, healers, and Witches, everyone agrees that the alpha state is the doorway to creative psychic work. Some methods include drumming, chanting, dancing, deep breathing, music, and holding the body in specific postures. The method I teach as part of the Science of Witchcraft is called the "Crystal Count-down," a visualization process combining color and number.

At this point, cast your spell, do a projection, charge an object, or perform whatever magical work you have planned.

Close your eyes, take a few deep breaths, and picture either a red seven or the number seven against a red background. Hold it for a few seconds, and then picture an orange six. Proceed downward through a yellow five, green four, blue three, purple two, orchid one. When your attention settles into orchid, say to yourself, "I am now in alpha, and everything I do will be accurate and correct, and this is so." Deepen the state even more by counting down from ten to one without any color component, and then repeat the suggestion as above.

At this point, cast your spell, do a projection, charge an object, or perform whatever magical work you have planned.

To return to ordinary consciousness, count slowly upward from one to seven. Colors are not necessary for the return. Take a few deep breaths, slowly becoming aware of your physical surroundings.

Casting a Circle

Because spells work with cosmic energy and because we view that energy as divine, we create sacred space by casting a circle around ourselves before casting a spell. In this way we put ourselves physically into a ring of magic, an environment filled with the very energy we work with.

There are formal and informal ways to cast a magic circle and create sacred space. Since many of the spells in this book are short, informal activities for you alone or you and your partner (as opposed to elaborate rituals involving a coven or large group of people intended to last for an entire evening), I will give you a quick and easy method of casting a magic circle.

Locate the four directions: east, south, west, and north. Stand facing north, go into alpha. With a wand, athame, or your index finger, draw a circle around yourself sunwise (clockwise), saying, "I cast this circle to protect me and to draw in only the energies and forces that are right for me and the most correct for my work." Then face each direction and invoke the spirits, elements, and powers of that direction as you know and honor them, beginning in the east. Say, for example, "I invoke the East, the spirits (or deities) of air/wind/sky/sound, etc. I invoke the South, the spirits (or deities) of fire/forge/hearth/light, etc. I invoke the West, the spirits (or deities) of water/oceans/rivers/wells, etc. I invoke the North, the spirits (or deities) of earth/field/forest/mountain/cavern, etc." The spirits or powers you name can be specific Gods and Goddesses or more general terms like these. You can also invoke animal spirits such as birds in the East, fur-bearing animals in the South, fish and water creatures in the West, and the horned and hoofed animals in the North. You will then be inside a magic circle and working in sacred space.

When the spell or ritual is over, open the circle by drawing your athame, wand, or finger counterclockwise, beginning in the North as before. Say, "I send this circle into the universe to do my bidding. The circle is undone but not broken."

If you are in a setting where you cannot physically cast the circle, you can do so mentally by visualizing the directions and a perfect circle of light.

Charging an Object

Charging an object or magical tool is a method of transferring energy from you (or from the universe through you) into an article to be used for magical purposes. Hold the object in your hand, go into alpha, and see in your mind's eye the aura already around the object. Auras appear differently to different people. They may look like light, color, radiation, mist, a shimmering field, or some combination of these. Wipe away any chaotic, harmful, or unwanted energy in the object with a sweeping motion of one hand a few inches above the object, saying, "I neutralize any incorrect energy in this (name the object)." Then visualize your aura and/or cosmic energy entering the cleared energy field of the object. Notice its aura becoming brighter, sharper, denser, more intense. Say, "I charge this (name it) to be a source of power and energy for (state its purpose: love, healing, protection, happiness, etc.). I ask that this be correct and for the good of all. And so it is."

Shapeshifting

Witches' spells often involve shapeshifting, which can occur on the level of consciousness, at the level of the aura, and, in more advanced stages, on the physical level. The spells in this book require only shapeshifting for the purpose of participating in the consciousness of another object. It is a basic principle of magic that everything is alive and responsive, so we expect everything, even rocks, fire, water, and wind, to have a state of consciousness. Shapeshifting techniques allow the energy patterns of our consciousness to merge with the energy patterns of something else.

In a state of shared consciousness, then, we can influence the object or allow it to influence us by sharing its wisdom or power with us. In this way Merlin trained the young Arthur by shapeshifting techniques. He turned the future king into fish, birds, and animals to learn their secret knowledge. In the process, Arthur also gained some of their power and energy.

Love magic sometimes requires shifting consciousness so that it aligns with that of another person. In so doing, energy is shared and exchanged, and by means of your will, you can direct and guide the other toward your desired end. The spells never neutralize another person's free will. They never deprive another of his or her own independent consciousness. When you say that you do a spell for the good of all and to harm no one, you automatically include the intention not to harm another's integrity and independence.

The goal of many love spells is broader than simply influencing another person to fall in love with you. Some spells merge your consciousness with another's so he or she can influence you as well. Then with greater mutual cooperation and understanding, the two of you become one on a psychic level where it is easier to fall in love, heal and protect each other, build a life together, share the good times and hopefully ward off the bad. In other words, shapeshifting of consciousness is a way to pool psychic resources. Love always seeks to merge with the beloved, with or without magic, such as when you find yourself constantly thinking about your lover. When done correctly, love magic can help that natural attraction along, strengthen it, make it more satisfying and productive.

Here is a method for shaping consciousness.

1. Place your attention upon the object. This is not the same as holding an image of the object in your mind. Consciously direct your attention out from you, like a beam of light, in the direction of the object.

2. After a few seconds, put your consciousness into the object. In other words, begin to think and feel as you imagine the object thinks and feels. When you do this with inanimate objects such as rocks, leaves, or clouds, you might have to suspend your disbelief if your worldview does not allow for inanimate objects to have consciousness, but even people who just "play along," as it were, find that the results of their shapeshifting are just as powerful as for people with animistic belief systems.

3. Continue to keep your consciousness in the object until you notice your awareness "flickering." You will know this is happening when there are moments of *imagining* that you are thinking and feeling like the object, interspersed with moments when you are *actually experiencing what the object is experiencing.* It may take practice to reach this stage. In time you will know the difference between step two and step three and appreciate this flickering mode of consciousness in which you share awareness with the object. When you get proficient at shapeshifting, the "flicker" will steady into longer periods of identification with the object, but you will never lose awareness of yourself or the ability to shift quickly

back into your own state of consciousness when you will it.

4. To return to your own consciousness, become aware of some part of your own body (such as your face or a part of your face) and focus your attention on it, allowing it to dominate your awareness. As this happens, your identification with the object will fade and you will be back in your normal state of consciousness.

It is often said that the most powerful effects of any spell are on the one who casts it. This is especially true of shapeshifting spells, but the object you "become" will never replace who you are. You will always retain the core of your own integrity and being. Some percentage of you will always remain you.

With these four techniques you are now ready to begin some actual love spells.

Rituals to Begin the Magic

PEOPLE living a magical life surround themselves with reminders of the energy-filled world in which they live. Their homes, clothing, yard, car, workplace, even meals, reflect their belief in a magical universe. The difference between the person who occasionally practices magic and the person who leads a magical life can be seen in the pervasiveness of magic in the lifestyle and environment of the latter. The following six rituals are intended to "set up your life" or get you started on the royal road of magic, which I hope leads to a more fulfilling love life. Each ritual focuses on a key component of magic: charms, incantations, altars, power spots, the elements of nature, and magical brews. Each is a love spell in its own right to empower you for spells and rituals to follow. If you are new to magic, use these simple spells to "get your feet wet" before plunging into the more complex spells of later chapters.

This book is not a "program" of love magic, but it could be used that way. Beginners in the Craft may want to proceed through the chapters in the order they are presented, but keep in mind that you do not need to do every spell or ritual in the book, although reading through them all will give you a sense of the richness and variety of magic.

When it comes to magic, be flexible and be creative. Remember that the word *Witch* comes from the old Saxon word *Wych* and the Old English word *Wicce,* both meaning to turn, bend, or shape. This is the heart of old European Witchcraft as we practice it today. While every culture has magic, our Craft is rooted in the Western European magical traditions that evolved along with the very word itself: Witchcraft—the power to change and transform ourselves, others, and situations for the good of all and to harm none. So whether you are a Witch or not, whether your ancestry derives from Western Europe or not, I invite you to share in this ancient heritage and change or reshape any of the spells and rituals in this book. The most powerful spells are the ones we create ourselves. The most potent love is that which we turn, bend, and shape from our own hearts.

Ritual I: *A Personal Love Charm*

In quest tales, heroes are usually given magical talismans charged by a wizard or sorceress to protect and empower them on their journeys. Since you are committing yourself to a journey for love, a fitting charm or talisman will strengthen your resolve when you, like the hero of myth and folklore, encounter obstacles. This spell to charge a love charm can be an expression of your seriousness about changing the course of your love life—to attract, enhance, or end a relationship. The charm can be used as a personal power tool in other love rituals or carried with you to bring love into your life during the day. Or you might want to carry it only when you go on dates or for times together. You can charge a similar charm or something else altogether as a love gift for your partner.

Here are some suggestions:

♦ a clear crystal or precious stone, especially rose quartz, possibly in the form of jewelry
♦ a special ring consecrated to make you a better lover, the circle being a symbol of wholeness and perfection
♦ a pressed flower (rose or violet), possibly from a bouquet that was given as an expression of love, or one you picked on a special day
♦ a small piece of wood (willow, rowan, or applewood) on which you carve love runes, your own personal symbols, or the initials of your lover
♦ a nut (acorn for the fertility God) or seed (apple seed for the Goddess) to remind you that love is always a matter of hidden potential and growth

RITUAL II: *LOVE INCANTATION*

Ancient magic was often word magic. Words of power, spoken with courage and confidence in preliterate societies, later written down or inscribed, have always been key ingredients in spells. Today we live in a society where the spoken and written word proliferates and bombards and dulls our senses. Words seem cheap, and modern magic-workers often overlook the power of the word. Spells are written or spoken carelessly. How alien a Celtic bard or storyteller would feel in the world of modern magic where wordcraft is not taken seriously!

Fortunately, being in love can remind us of the power of the word. Saying "I love you" to someone for the first time, for example, is an act fraught with mystery, wonder, and danger. How will she take it? Am I saying it too soon? Should I wait? For what? To let him say it first? Saying those three little words is a highly charged act of power. It brings consequences.

Love letters and phone calls depend on the power of the word. Without the physical presence of the other supporting us and responding to what we say with facial expressions and body language, we are reliant upon the word alone. No wonder that before we call or write, we think over what we want to say, and choose our words carefully because word-power alone links us with the one we love.

Lovers also feel drawn to keeping diaries and writing poetry. On a psychological level, these activities help people evaluate relationships, reflect on the great movements of emotion and desire that course through their lives, and make decisions for the future.

Most spells require words of some kind, either spoken or written. The more often you formally put your intentions into words, the easier the practice becomes. And practice is absolutely necessary. Begin now by writing a short four-line poem or incantation to yourself asking for the wisdom to discern what true love requires or the courage to open up your life to love. Both goals are extremely worthwhile because the greatest obstacles to love are ignorance of what real love entails and the crowded, sometimes selfish, lifestyle with no room for love.

You don't have to be a great poet to write a Craft poem, a verse or chant used in rituals. The poet-within is really the child-within, who knows spontaneously how to create a simple verse of great power. Many of the old nursery rhymes, silly as they might sound today, were originally magical chants. If possible, write your poem in a traditional rhythm and rhyme that can tap into deeper levels of consciousness, unlocking memories and ancient knowledge helpful for magical work. Don't worry if the rhyme sounds trite or clichéd, and the beat is singsong. Your poem is not a work of literature; it is a work of magic.

Here is a verse that you might use as a model:

> From morning to noon, and noon to dusk
> The power of love surrounds me.
> With scent of flower and herb and musk
> Love's power ignites and grounds me.

Carry the poem with you, or tape it to your mirror, or keep it in some special place, perhaps under your pillow.

RITUAL III: *LOVE ALTAR*

Every Witch has an altar of some kind in the home or in a yard, garden, or nearby woods. An old desk, a lowboy, a buffet, or a nightstand can serve as an indoor altar. Usually the four elements—air, fire, water, earth—are represented in the four directions respectively. A statue or picture of the Mother Goddess and her Son, the Horned God, an incense burner, candles, crystals and other sacred stones, complete the arrangement. Personal items can also be included. Each altar is a unique power spot and reflects the interests, personality, and tradition of the Witch who creates it.

In my backyard I have a beautiful English garden where I

grow flowers and herbs. The ground is strewn with crystals and magical objects. I constructed a special altar there near a miniature maple tree using a round piece of marble I bought in a kitchen shop, the kind used in rolling out dough. I placed it on four large pieces of rose quartz. On the altar are a bowl, a heart-shaped piece of wood, and a bottle tightly sealed with love potion. On occasions I place in the bowl a favorite cookie, a piece of apple, or some strawberries to attract love. On moonlit evenings I might add a small pink votive candle to let its light mingle with the stars and the scent of flowers and the night mist.

You can add special objects charged for love magic to your present altar or create a separate love altar altogether. If you are not a Witch, you might transform the table or dresser where you keep your lover's photo into a more power-filled place by making it a kind of shrine. I have a very simple love altar of this kind on one side of the dresser in my bedroom.

Here are some simple ways to create an altar:

♦ Add a bud vase with two fresh flowers and replace them as needed, one for you and one for your sweetheart. Use roses or any flower with special significance for the two of you.

♦ Place a special red or pink candle on the altar or near the photograph, and light it when you talk on the phone, write a letter, or dress and groom yourself before meeting your partner.

♦ Keep the love poem from the preceding spell rolled up or folded on the altar, or laid out flat so you can read it.

♦ After buying your lover a gift, magically charge the present and place it on the altar for a few days before you give it.

♦ Arrange on the altar other keepsakes, mementos, or love gifts, from either your current partner or past relationships.

♦ If you currently have no mate, you can still create an altar with these objects. But instead of a photograph as the central point, use an erotic picture or painting or a piece of sculpture, perhaps depicting a God or Goddess of Love. Bride magazines are good sources for romantic photos: weddings, rings, flowers, gifts, honeymoons. Select photos that turn your thoughts and feelings to love and companionship.

RITUAL IV: *ROMANTIC POWER SPOTS*

Witches and magic-workers are drawn to places of power. Lovers are drawn to erotic or romantic places. As a Witch and a lover, you can have them both! Here are some suggestions for transforming romantic places into power spots.

Go to a place you associate with love or romance, such as an art museum or gallery with erotic or romantic paintings or sculptures, a lovers' lane, places you have gone to with former lovers, even stores or shops at your local mall that display images of beauty, health, strength, glamour, or romance. When you consciously acknowledge and admire the beauty and power of any image, it becomes a channel of that power and energy. The image might be that of a simple park bench that has special meaning for you, a painting of two lovers, or a boutique that sells sexy clothing. Draw the image into your consciousness as you would any symbol, and let the qualities it represents resonate with your intentions. Magic and power can be found in any place.

To increase the power of a romantic spot, you can perform ritual activities such as: drawing in the love energy you find there; charging talismans, amulets, or love gifts; doing projections; and writing in your diary or composing a letter to your lover.

RITUAL V: *MORNING DEW RITUAL*

Robert Frost wrote, "Earth's the right place for love, I can't imagine where it might go better." Witches might paraphrase this: "Earth's the right place for spells, we can't imagine where they might go better." The earth's elements—wind, fire, water, stone—are intrinsically part of Witchcraft. We use the elements in spells because they encapsulate the energies of the physical universe. Everything material contains and reflects spiritual power.

Dew is an especially magical form of moisture, appearing overnight while the earth dreams. Some folk traditions call it "Faerie rain." Part of its power lies in its mysterious origins. Does it fall from the sky like rain? Does it rise up from the earth like mist? The scientific explanation, of course, is that dew is formed by both—the air and the earth—since it is condensation that results from certain combinations of temperatures in the air and on the ground. Dew appeals to a Witch's imagination because we are fond of situations that are "betwixt and between," such as twilight, cliff edges, seashores, any rim or crack, a mirror's image, a doorway, or a place of fog and mist. Dew in the morning light is one of these. Whether you subscribe to the world of science, temperature, and condensation, or you favor the world of Faerie and magic, dew is mysterious and special in its beauty and fragility.

For this ritual, rise before dawn and go outdoors, naked if possible and if it's warm enough. Spend a few moments feeling the wet, dewy grass beneath your bare feet. As the new day's light begins to brighten the sky, pick several leaves or blades of grass that are laden with dew. Look at them closely. Observe the daylight glistening in the moisture on them. Put your consciousness into the drops of dew. Then offer the leaves to the four directions, casting an informal circle around you as you do so. Then face east. Hold the leaves up to the sky and say:

"With this Faerie dew I anoint my head that it may be filled with loving thoughts." (Brush the leaves across your forehead.) "With this Faerie dew I anoint my heart that it may overflow with feelings of love." (Brush the leaves across your chest.) "With this Faerie dew I anoint my sex (call it what you call it) that it may enjoy the pleasures of lovemaking." (Brush the leaves across your genitals).

Then lie down and roll around in the dew for a morning bath. Let the rising sun or the morning air dry your body, or go back inside and let it dry naturally. Keep the leaves for remembering magic. Collect some of the dew in a bottle and dab some on your loved one or save it for other magical work.

Ritual VI: *Brews and Blends*

Witches brew various ingredients to make magical potions, and we blend the right combinations of herbs to make incense and philters. Potions and philters can be created and used for love or for other purposes, such as success, health, prosperity. Many recipes come from old family commonplace books handed down from generation to generation and from the Books of

Shadows that Witches keep, adding to them as they develop new spells, rituals, brews, and blends.

When the moon, sun, and Venus are in proper alignment, I go to my magic cabinet and take out the oils, candles, and herbs to make love potions. I am doing this more and more lately since the world needs all the love we can generate. Some potions I sell, others I give as gifts to friends.

A few years ago I gave Susan, a friend in New York City, a love potion when she was having difficulty meeting people. I charged it specifically so that she would meet someone who would be "right" for her, provided it would be for the good of all concerned. Two days after she started wearing it, she was invited to a music club in Vermont where she met a wonderful, charming, talented, sexy musician. They spoke briefly that evening before he left to go off with other friends. Susan returned to New York, wondering if she would ever see him again. She kept wearing the potion, and two months later received a letter from him saying that he had been trying to track her down since that night. Today they are happily married.

Here are three easy recipes, one for love oil, one for love potion, the third for love incense.

Homemade Love Oil

You will need:

> 1 cup almond oil
> 5 drops Cerridwen oil
> 5 willow leaves
> 5 apple seeds

On a Friday during a waxing moon, create a magical space around your stove by casting a circle. Place the seeds and willow leaves in the almond oil and add the Cerridwen oil. Warm the oil, but do not let it boil. Let it cool and pour it into a jar, and label it "Love Oil." Place the oil in a secret place and take it out only when you are going to use it for a love spell.

Love Potion

If you do not have easy access to herbal oils, here is a water-based potion. You will need:

>   2 cups springwater
>   3 tablespoons salt
>   1 teaspoon basil
>   3 rose petals
>   1 teaspoon vanilla extract
>   1 enamel pan
>   1 pink candle

Charge all the ingredients in a magic circle. Simmer for two minutes while visualizing love coming into your life and see a pink aura around and in the potion. Light the candle and project your thoughts for love. When the potion has cooled, tightly cap it in a bottle and wear it.

Homemade Love Incense

You will need herbs, spices, and oils, which you can select from the lists in Chapter 10:

sawdust or talcum powder or powdered herbs or spices of your choice (use one or a combination of the three in equal amounts)

saltpeter

a few drops of essential oils from the herbs ruled by Venus, Mars, or the moon (see Chapter 10)

Mix the ingredients together, then charge the incense. Burn it during romantic times with your lover.

The Power Lover Within

I<small>N</small> I<small>RELAND</small> many people still value and protect the old Faerie customs and practice the folk magic of their ancestors. Perhaps more than elsewhere Ireland is still a place where Craft magic and power live on in the lives of ordinary people whether they think of themselves as Witches or not. In County Armagh the gateposts of a farmstead are sometimes referred to as the "man and woman" of the farmhouse. According to local tradition, villagers put the first two plates of mashed potatoes on top of the posts at Samhain, October 31, so the man and woman will not go hungry. A visitor separates the man and woman by opening the gate, passing between them, and then reunites them as the gate closes.

There is a great mystery in this ordinary event and much magical and psychological truth. The old Irish peasant custom reflects something vitally important about the human psyche and critically important about love magic: The cooperation and celebration of the male and female principles within each of us leads to self-esteem and psychic wholeness. Both love and magic depend on this.

Although every person is either biologically male or female, each human psyche contains both masculine and feminine components. This chapter will show you how to recognize and appreciate the "opposite sex" aspects of your psyche and how to use this knowledge in magic. It will also help you love yourself more completely—self-esteem and a healthy self-love being requirements for mature, sound relationships.

THE MAN WITHIN, THE WOMAN WITHIN

Each male psyche contains an archetype of the divine feminine, and each female psyche an archetype of the divine masculine. (The great Swiss analyst Carl Jung called them *anima* and *animus,* the feminine and masculine forms of the Latin word for soul.) I use the word *divine* here intentionally to refer to these Inner Partners because they display a numinous power we associate with a God or Goddess, and I believe they deserve the same awe and respect usually reserved for a divine being who knows our inner realms. In short, we are the God and Goddess.

In Western magical traditions, the Hermetic Law of Gender states that everything, not just animals and human beings, contains a male and female principle, and that one of the keys to unlocking the magical power in any created thing is to work with and unite these two complementary forces. To enter the farmhouse of magic, so to speak, we must pass between the two gateposts of the masculine and feminine, pay tribute to both the man and woman within, and if it happens to be Samhain, leave some mashed potatoes for them!

Magic, as we have said, is about shifting consciousness, and the anima and the animus represent two different types of consciousness. To be powerful magic-workers, we must energize and bring the two out. The same is true for becoming great lovers: we must activate that Inner Opposite to acquire the self-esteem of a totally integrated human being. If you are heterosexual, knowing about your own Inner Opposite will help in understanding the "otherness" of your partner; if you are homosexual, knowing the demands and the gifts of your Inner Opposite will help you appreciate a same-sex lover, whose Inner Opposite is, of course, the same gender as your own opposite.

The patterns of consciousness we call the anima and animus, however, are not male and female in a strictly biological sense, as when science points out that every human being contains both male and female genes, chromosomes, and hormones. *Feminine* and *masculine* are more accurate terms for the anima and animus, rather than *female* and *male,* because these patterns of consciousness are as much culturally determined as they are shaped by biology. Each human being is born either male or female, but each *becomes* masculine or feminine, qualities greatly conditioned by culture.

In the Western world masculine consciousness is defined along these lines: It favors linear thinking and logic; planned action; physical force; analysis; fertilization; ego-consciousness; individuality; separation. It focuses on the polarity in situations and things, and develops a dualistic, "either–or" point of view. The masculine emphasizes the role people play in structuring human life.

Feminine consciousness is viewed differently. It favors cyclical thinking and intuition; spontaneous action; the ability to

wait, trust, yield, and allow; synthesis; formation and nur-
turence; the unconscious; relationship and wholeness. It focuses on the unity of opposites and develops a unifying, "both–
and" point of view. The feminine emphasizes the role of nature
in shaping human life.

These two modes of consciousness appear to be polar opposites. If it were not for the fact that each of us contains that
opposite within, we would probably never manage to understand, much less get along with, the opposite sex! Some lovers
subscribe to this, seeing an eternal "battle of the sexes" with
neither side ever understanding, winning over, or subduing the
other. At best, they hope for treaties, stalemates, or temporary
bouts of exhaustion. Witches never subscribe to that position
totally. As magic-workers, as shapeshifters, as diviners who
peer into the hearts of all things, we know it is possible to
understand the opposite sex. Magic is also defined as the art of
being able to communicate with the inner, spiritual powers in
nature, ourselves, and other human beings.

Masculine and feminine energies, therefore, have never been
formidable adversaries for people versed in the magical sciences. Gender is just one application of the Law of Polarity,
reminding us that everything contains its opposite. Each pair of
opposites challenges us to find the point of union, the common
ground where both poles participate as full and equal partners.
From a Witch's point of view, the masculine and feminine
modes of consciousness parallel the solar and lunar mysteries.
Solar consciousness, like the masculine, is bright, penetrating,
indomitable. Its often harsh brilliance allows us to appreciate
the smallest of details. It illuminates and reveals very important
differences and distinctions for human endeavors. The feminine
lunar consciousness, on the other hand, is gentle, subtle, indi-
rect. Its softer light blurs edges, and objects melt into each

other. Moonlight gives a sense of wholeness and the mysteriousness behind existence. Lunar experiences call for intuition, imagination, and speculation, rather than logic and submission to fact.

MEETING YOUR INNER PARTNER

Meeting your Inner Partner (your anima or animus) is a first step in self-love and a vital foundation for loving another human being. If you want to give your whole self to the person you love, self-knowledge regarding your inner psyche is of vital importance. You can go into relationships secure in knowing who you are and what you have to give. The ritual exercise that follows, like ancient initiation rites into the mysteries of love, will introduce you to the feminine or masculine within your self.

In both men and women, the Inner Partner tends to be hidden, unacknowledged, possibly even feared and suppressed because it appears to contradict images of the "real man" or the "real woman" based on societal norms. A journey to encounter your Inner Opposite, therefore, will be a quest to find and free the Man Within or the Woman Within from the prison of social stereotypes and the psychic guards that keep it there. In our society, for example, it is still a social taboo for a man to cry in public, even when some inner sorrow prompts it. Knowledge that all human beings cry and that it has nothing to do with masculinity or feminity, knowledge derived from dialogue with one's Inner Partner, can be liberating. The more you know how both the masculine and feminine operate in you, the more you will be able to view your behavior in human terms, not just as society conditions it.

Every man or woman's journey through life parallels the epic journey of adventure found in the world's great myths. The hero's quest for truth, power, or love reflects our own search for the meaning of life and those treasures, such as love, that make life worth living. Nonetheless, each individual must discover the elements of the quest unique to him or her. My description of the journey to your Inner Partner, therefore, is a general outline or map of the psychic terrain. As you embark on your personal quest, your journey may veer from my structure. Do not be alarmed. Journey to wherever your Inner Partner is hidden, meet him or her, and engage in a dialogue similar to the one I suggest below. (Remember that your Inner Partner will appear as the opposite sex: a woman if you're a man; a man if you're a woman.)

Since the psychic journey requires you to shift consciousness into alpha, you will not be able to read the guidelines while making the journey. Therefore, I suggest you read through them several times, fixing the simple pattern of the journey firmly in your mind. In this way you will be free to enter deeply into the journey, allow for spontaneous adventures, and still make it back. You may want to reflect on the description of the journey for a day or two, before actually doing the meditation.

Begin by sitting or lying down. Get comfortable, close your eyes, take a few deep breaths, count yourself into alpha. When your attention settles into orchid, your journey will begin.

You are standing at the edge of a lake beneath a full moon. The dark water shimmers with the moon's reflection. You hear it lapping on the shore. You are calm, self-assured, ready for adventure.

You have two choices for crossing the lake: a boat with a mysterious, silent figure, either male or female, sitting at the oars; or a white swan—the Celtic symbol of the Goddess—who will lead you across the water. Both rower and swan know the way to the Island.

As you cross the lake, riding in the boat or gliding with the swan, you pass through a mist illuminated by the light of the moon. You journey for a short time through folds of mist and moonlight, and emerge in view of a dark island. You reach the shore and walk up to the edge of a dense forest, knowing that somewhere in or beyond the forest is the castle where your Inner Partner waits for you. The forest is thick and threatening, but you spot a path and enter it. As you proceed, you get a strong premonition that your Inner Partner knows you have arrived on the Island and eagerly awaits you. You may even hear bells, chimes, or birdsong that call you and encourage your progress. At two different places on the path, you will encounter one of the two Guardians of the castle, who will attempt to prevent you from reaching it: one Guardian will be a human figure, the other an animal figure. It is your task to outwit, sneak past, or bind these Guardians with a cocoon of white light spun around them like strands of silk. Or use what-ever tools, weapons, or magical devices your imagination can create to neutralize their power. Do not destroy them. All things serve a purpose, and all things can be transformed. Who knows but that these Guardians may become allies on another journey.

After passing the Guardians, enter the castle and search through it. Notice the interior, the various rooms, passageways, materials, and objects that are there. Your Inner Partner will be in a high tower, a deep magical dungeon, or some other hidden chamber in the Castle. No one else lives in the Castle. There is no Lord or Lady. It is empty except for your Inner Partner, and now you.

When you find your Inner Partner, initiate a dialogue with

him or her. These questions (as well as others that occur to you) should make up the discussion:

What is your name? Or what do you want to be called?

How can I (or we together) break the enchantment keeping you here and depriving me of your wisdom and power in ordinary reality?

What task can I do for you here on the Island or in the Castle?

What changes in my life would make me a more attractive and effective lover?

Do you have a spirit guide or power animal for me?

When you finish your conversation, make plans for a return visit. Then say good-bye, and return to the lake shore (the Guardians will still be quelled!), where your boat or swan waits to take you back across the lake, through the mist and moonlight, to where you began.

Now that you have begun a relationship with your Inner Partner, you must nurture it. On return visits, you might find the same Guardians (or new ones) reemerge to thwart you once again, or other unexpected obstacles block your way. On the other hand, some return trips through the forest might be relatively uneventful. Sometimes a new enchantment holds your Inner Partner hostage, and you must release him or her from it. (In psychological terms, it requires vigilance and effort to keep the anima/animus available as a conscious resource.) No two journeys are ever exactly the same.

As you would with other spirit guides, nurture your relationship with your Inner Partner by periodic meditations or journeys, by being mindful of the Inner Partner's presence during the day, by reflecting on what you have learned from him or her and trying to put it into practice. Being of the opposite sex, your Inner Partner will tend to view situations in a different light, giving you an alternative perspective to work out difficulties and problems more effectively. On subsequent visits, tell your Inner Partner about your recent experiences in the form of a story, and ask for advice or suggestions on how to handle them better in the future. Inner psychic figures can make their presence known spontaneously and in subtle ways. We do not always need to journey to the Otherworld each time we need inner help.

There are other formal ways to access the Inner Partner. The meditations and rituals in the remainder of this chapter are structured to tap into the androgynous levels of the psyche and call forth strong archetypal images of warriors and magicians that unite the feminine and masculine energy of the unconscious.

THE EROTIC ANDROGYNE

In the first half of the twentieth century, Hollywood and the advertising industry began creating "ideal" masculine and feminine standards of beauty, and many young people grew up dreaming they would fall in love with someone who matched them. In reality, human attraction is more varied and far more interesting. No hard and fast rules govern falling in love and sexual attraction. Some very masculine men, for example, prefer women with some masculine qualities, and some very feminine women go for men with feminine traits. Opposites can attract just as easily as similarities. Couples who live together long enough begin to resemble each other in looks, voice, values, and ways of doing things, no matter how different they were when they first met. In terms of physical "beauty," some very good-looking people are attracted to very plain-looking partners. All this implies something far more mysterious and magical than the simple, automatic bonding of the idealized masculine and feminine stereotypes created by the media. Clearly, beauty is in the eye of the beholder.

In the 1960s, the androgynous look and personality reemerged in the West after several centuries of suppression. Standards of beauty and sexuality loosened up from the older media stereotypes, allowing much more freedom and individuality, and probably a good deal more honesty on the part of many people. Once again, people can be more authentically themselves, and not feel pressured to fit a predetermined mold, or feel ashamed if they don't. Long hair on men, short hair on women, shaved heads on both, unisex clothing, jobs and careers less restricted by gender, individuals developing their natural talents and interests regardless of whether they have been traditionally labeled masculine or feminine. Mixing and matching of genders produces wonderfully creative and erotic styles —which brings us back to the need to recognize, understand, develop, and be proud of both our feminine and our masculine characteristics, whether physical, psychological, or spiritual.

Scrying the Androgyne

Scrying is the practice of gazing deeply and psychically at some object and seeing in it a pattern, movement, or change that imparts information about a question or issue. Tea leaves in the bottom of a cup, patterns in clouds or water, shadows in the flicker of firelight, visions in a crystal ball or mirror, can all be scryed. In Celtic tradition, scrying was called "the sight" or the "second sight." Some people are better at this than others (as is true of most skills), but everyone can scry to some extent. In this section you will learn how to scry into your own nature and discover the androgynous qualities of your psyche.

Psychologists report that when our opposite-gender qualities remain submerged and unacknowledged, we tend to project them onto someone of the opposite sex. We look for, or imagine, the unacknowledged parts of ourselves in others. We can then easily fall in love with someone who embodies those qualities. Disappointment usually follows because we expect our loved ones to supply the gifts of gender we have not found in ourselves. It is usually asking too much of someone to fill in our psychic gaps for us. Such love affairs tend to break up. If, on the other hand, we can satisfy our "soul" needs from within, from our own inner resources, we become well-rounded individuals, free to fall in love with others for what they are, not for what they can supply for us. We are freed from the compulsion to make people into what we want them to be. They can be themselves. We can be ourselves. Love usually thrives better that way.

Here is a method for scrying the androgynous qualities in your own nature. Take an ordinary mirror, or a dark, smoky Witch's mirror, and sit comfortably in front of it. Darken the room and place a lighted candle between you and the mirror. Burn some incense to alter the ambience of the room and to turn your attention inward. The resins benzoin and copal are good scents for burning, or the herb dittany of Crete, all of which bring visions.

Close your eyes and count yourself into alpha. Sit in a meditative state for a few moments with your eyes closed, focusing your inner attention on nothing in particular. Then open your eyes and look at your reflection in the mirror. Gaze deeply into your countenance. First, scan different parts of your face for masculine and feminine qualities. You might notice, for example, that your eyelashes are long, your jawline square, forehead rugged, lips petite, cheekbones smooth, chin dainty. Our society has stereotyped the qualities "long, square, rugged, petite, smooth, and dainty" as either masculine or feminine, and the conscious mind tends to see things in terms of opposites, so it should not be difficult to find different signs of gender in your face. Most people can do so.

Next, gaze behind your face at the "you" behind the physical expression. Notice how your soul shines through your eyes. Study this "inner you" reflected in your face, and discover its androgynous nature. What parts of it seem masculine, which feminine? What you are viewing on a physical level are the spiritual qualities of your Inner Partner, qualities representing energy that can empower your relationships, your lovemaking, and your magic.

As you scry, keep your mind free of value judgments regarding what you see. Try not to label any quality as good or bad, strong or weak, acceptable or unacceptable. Remember that the Law of Polarity tells us that everything contains its opposite, so whatever seems "bad" or "weak" to you also has positive strengths. Often our value judgments are made in a particular context blinding us to the complementary qualities also present, and only later when the context changes do we revise those judgments. The purpose of this exercise is not to judge, but to notice and appreciate the various dimensions of your androgyny.

Sometimes we see in someone else a marvelous combination of soul qualities we lack blended with the very qualities that make us "us." This discovery may come in a flash, as on a first encounter, or gradually, like scrying, over time. Such a person may turn out to be a "soulmate." But we ought to pro ceed with caution and not mistake the euphoria of recognition for lust that then leads to sex. It often happens that sex destroys wonderful platonic relationships. When you really discover a soulmate, protect that person as you would your own life. The love binding soulmates is usually communication, not sex. In a soulmate we find someone with whom we can really talk, open our hearts and minds, share our deepest thoughts and feelings. Treasure that bond and be wary of turning it into a sexual thrill that might prove to be as thin as gossamer.

WARRIORS AND LOVERS

Celtic customs reflected a remarkable appreciation for the androgynous nature of human beings. The sexes enjoyed considerable equality in marriage customs, property rights, legal status, as well as economic and political activities. Also, the widespread acceptance of homosexuality and bisexuality indicates a tolerant, open definition of male and female roles. The importance of women warriors and rulers, and their role in training young men as warriors, further suggests that the Celtic imagination did not draw very rigid lines between the polarities of masculine and feminine. And yet, judging from the wonderful tales of love and romance that have come down to us in Celtic folklore, as well as the Celtic-inspired literature on courtly love, the freer sex roles did not interfere with heterosexual relationships. In fact, the equality and the respect shown both sexes may have actually strengthened heterosexual relationships and given them that sensual and mystical blend typical of Celtic folk romance.

We can learn a lot about androgyny from two Celtic folk heroes: Lancelot, the favored knight of Arthur's Round Table, and Scathach, a woman warrior who trained many young Celtic boys in the arts of war. I believe both characters are representations of the anima and animus, as manifested in an inner warrior archetype. When the warrior archetype operates with both feminine and masculine energies, we are more evenly balanced. We act from a position of strength and gentleness; we are decisive and fair; we are, in short, chivalrous. Our magic, our lives, and our relationships are infused with "soul"—anima and animus. As we are spiritual warriors, our actions spring from an ethic of strength, intellectual cunning, and high moral purpose.

Training the Androgyne Warrior

Scathach was a Witch and a warrior, skilled in both magic and the martial arts. She was known as the "woman who strikes fear" into the hearts of her enemies. A goddess figure whose realm was the Isle of Skye off Scotland, she trained young men in the arts of war, as well as in hunting, tracking, and the chase. Only the most resolute apprentices survived the journey to Scathach's island, however, because they had to cross a swaying bridge that flung unworthy initiates into the water.

The perilous bridge and other difficult and paradoxical tasks were typical of Scathach's training. Women warriors often sent initiates on quests and then put barriers in their path, often themselves, in the shape of beasts or evil warriors. Their methods of pedagogy created obstacles to test the young men's wit and skill, but ultimately they would emerge from the tasks stronger and wiser warriors.

The Irish hero Cuchulainn crossed Scathach's bridge with the "salmon's leap": one jump to the center of the bridge, and a second to the other side, demonstrating metaphorically the leap of faith to enter the realm of the feminine. Logical, rational considerations must be set aside. Often the direct lunge is the only way into the territory of the unconscious. In mythic terms Cuchulainn must trust his heart. A woman can teach him how, for women are never as terrified of the unconscious, when trained in women's mysteries and when their innate rapport with the night, the dark, the womb, and the Great Mother has not been ruptured by a patriarchal value system that holds these feminine secrets in contempt.

Scathach taught Cuchulainn the ways of the warrior and also the mysteries of sex. As the legends put it, she offered him "the friendship of her thighs." The Celtic woman warrior was known to be a fiercely erotic lover even as she could be a formidable foe. Even today, a woman's physical strength and martial skills need not be a barrier to her eroticism. An androgynous blend of sword and lace, chain and silk, the tough and the tender, has tremendous erotic power. It taps into some deep sense of excitement in most men and many women, even though the image is at odds with the patriarchal view of women as weak and powerless. Nevertheless, physical strength, dexterity, skillful cunning, and unflinching determination are qualities that can improve a woman's performance on the battlefield as well as in the bedroom.

Meditation: Go into alpha and see yourself on a wide plain where a medieval battle is taking place. There is a great clash of arms, swords, lances, and maces. You see fierce hand-to-hand combat. As you peer through the dust and smoke, you notice that the armies are made up of both men and women. They appear to be evenly matched.

Stand outside the fray for a few moments, and let your consciousness change into that of a warrior, ready to enter the battle. As you watch for the best moment to throw yourself into the fight, you realize you don't know the first thing about being a medieval warrior! You turn to leave and see a tall, physically powerful woman behind you, holding a sword and a shield. Her hair is flaming red, her green eyes radiate confidence and boldness. She exudes both military and magical skills. With a flourish of her sword above her head, she causes the battle to vanish. The plain is now empty and quiet, except for you and her. As the two of you look at each other, your eyes seem to indicate that you both know why you are there. You are there to learn, she to train you as a warrior. She is Scathach.

Scathach leads you into a shaded glen where a shield and a sword wait for you. You pick them up and ask her what they *mean*. (In magical realms, everything has meaning, everything has a voice, everything is conscious and wants to tell us something.) Scathach will tell you what each means on both physical and spiritual levels. Listen to her carefully, and ask any questions that occur to you about the warrior spirit and ethic. She will explain to you the moral responsibility of being a warrior. After she has finished the lesson, she will show you how to use the sword and the shield. The two of you will practice sparring for a while until you grow tired. At that point, thank her for the lesson, and ask her if she suggests you return later for another. Then walk out of the glade onto the plain. Take a deep breath, and as you exhale, return to ordinary reality.

If you are a man, reflect upon how it feels to be apprenticed to Scathach, a woman who has the skills and knowledge traditionally associated with men. If you are a woman, take pride in learning from another woman the skills and knowledge that, throughout most of our history, have been a male's prerogative. Over the next few days, the warrior training you received will stay with you, and you will find yourself going about your activities with renewed vigor, enthusiasm, and self-esteem.

Self-esteem is not a destination but a way of traveling, each step along the journey strengthening us in the self-confidence that it is all right to be who we are. Self-doubts about whether we are acting like so-called real men or real women can weaken our trust in the value of androgyny. At such times it helps for a man to trust the woman within, and for a woman to trust the man within, who remind us that our androgynous nature, far from being a handicap, is a source of self-esteem.

Strengthening the Feminine: A Meditation for Men

Lancelot was the ideal knight and warrior, Arthur's best friend, Guinevere's champion and most passionate love. He was a valiant hero in numerous battles, jousts, and quests, and yet he was never a "man's man." He was foremost a "woman's man" whose androgynous qualities women found irresistible. From a woman's perspective, he was the ideal lover: he had physical beauty and charm; he played music and could speak enchanted words of poetry; he had an inner purity and a tough spirituality; he was both tender and strong. Not only did Lancelot make a great lover, he could be a woman's soulmate.

This blending of the feminine and masculine came from Lancelot's upbringing. He was known as Lancelot of the Lake because, according to an early tradition, he was raised by a lake Faerie, who gave him a magic ring with the power of breaking enchantments for anyone who looked at it. In later accounts Lancelot's Faerie teacher was called the Lady of the Lake. Whoever this mysterious woman or Goddess may have been, she clearly represented feminine consciousness (the lake is a classic feminine symbol and represents the many layers of consciousness, even to the depths of the unconscious). In psychological terms, Lancelot was well versed in the feminine side of his human nature, and drew strength and wisdom from the depths of the unconscious. He was unashamed to cultivate the feminine virtues women value in themselves. He was chivalrous.

Lancelot's power was paradoxical: He stood tall among the knights of the Round Table, praised for superior strength and prowess as a warrior, his strength and prowess tapping the feminine unconscious and the deep mysteries of women. Lancelot is a worthy ally for any man insecure about the softer side of his personality, for any man who doubts that masculinity can incorporate feminine consciousness.

Meditation: Darken the room or wait until night. Light a white candle. Burn incense in a cauldron or some other incense pot, and allow the scent and the drift of smoke to work its magic on your awareness. Go into alpha and gaze into the smoke. Become aware of how the candlelight and incense are changing the character of the room. Recite the following lines (or similar ones that you compose yourself):

> I am the wind that blows across the sea. I am the wild stag. I am the eagle on the cliff. I am swift as a hawk. I am a warrior of many battles. I am strong as a spear. I am the sharp point of a steel blade. I am the skin on the battle-calling drum. I am a string on a harp. I am the voice of poetry. I am the champion of the weak. I am the view from the highest mountain. I am the wisdom of the deepest well. I am the champion of the day and the night. I have been alive forever. There is nothing in which I have not been.

When you have recited these lines or similar ones, letting those with special meaning for you repeat themselves, and when your sense of time and place has shifted, see Lancelot's hand in the smoke of the incense. It firmly grasps a magnificent sword. On his finger is a magical ring. He extends his arm toward you so that you can see the ring while his hand tightens around the sword. Look at the ring closely, noting its design and the ornamentation. This is the ring given him by the Lady of the Lake. It has the power to break enchantments.

As you meditate upon the ring, draw into your awareness at least one doubt, worry, or insecurity about your masculinity. Ask Lancelot to free you from this negative enchantment once and for all. As you make the request, see the ring grow brighter, a cosmic light radiating from it toward you. The light's heat envelops your body until you, too, glow with this otherworldly sheen. Sit in the strength of the light for a few moments, and pull it inward with each deep breath. Let it energize your heart and lungs as you breathe, expanding the muscles around your chest and shoulders. After a while, the brightness begins to fade, and you see only the smoke of the incense.

Come back to ordinary consciousness by reciting one or two of the invocations above that seem appropriate, and end with the ancient Celtic poet Taliesin's two lines: "I have been alive forever. There is nothing in which I have not been."

Repeat this ritual whenever you have doubts about your masculinity or anytime you feel you have not acted like a "real man." In time, you will feel comfortable in Lancelot's presence. He will always break whatever enchantment prevents your feeling secure as a man. You may eventually ask him questions, seek advice, learn from him how to blend both masculine and feminine energies.

To consecrate yourself as a follower and companion of Lancelot, go on a quest for a ring embodying for you the qualities of Lancelot's magic ring. Buy it, then charge it to break enchantments that keep you from becoming the man that only you and your Inner Partner can be. Wear it with pride.

Reclaiming the Strong Feminine: A Meditation for Women

In a patriarchal culture, women's strengths and powers are often held in contempt. It is a sad fact, but true, that patriarchy devalues whatever is not identified as masculine and powerful. When men internalize these values and view other values as of little worth, their relationships with women, gay men, children, and nature—all of which fall outside the narrow definition of masculine—can range from uncomfortable to hostile and antagonistic. Many women also accept and internalize masculine-identified values, considering them to be superior to whatever is feminine, which they view as weak, subservient, and of lesser worth. These women are often confused and threatened by their own natural strengths and powers, especially if they have been brainwashed into thinking they have none or that such powers are wicked and dangerous.

Psychologists have discovered that when women dream about their "shadow" (those negative qualities we tend to keep suppressed below the level of awareness, unable to admit they are part of us), these dreams produce an amazing revelation. They are about Witches, sorceresses, fortune-tellers, Amazonian warriors, prostitutes! In other words, they are images of powerful, independent women who defy the "accepted" standards and morality of patriarchal culture. These "dream women" are strong, mysterious, and, above all, threatening to the male-oriented establishment. When a woman dreams of herself in these terms, she often awakes feeling nasty and "sinful." But not unwomanly! No matter how severely the Western patriarchal party line has skewed our image of ourselves as women, no matter how much we deny our intrinsic worth, dreams of ourselves as women of magical power tap into something genuinely, authentically, and eternally feminine. Something that is our birthright as women.

It has been said that a Witch is someone who practices magic "without a license." Our training, initiation procedures, and practices were illegal until the 1950s when the last laws against Witchcraft were repealed. Today Witchcraft is a legal religion in the United States. But still it is difficult to win acceptance in the minds and hearts of many people. Other clergy, doctors, pharmacists, and therapists all perform their brands of "magic" and are licensed to do so. As a Witch, I offer the same kinds of services: I heal, counsel, brew medicinal potions, and lead rituals for people who come to me for help or encouragement. In olden days I could have been branded a heretic for these activities, and in the worst of days, tortured and executed. We live in more enlightened times, but a Witch's magic is still held suspect by many people. It still emerges in women's dreams as something dangerous.

The following ritual is primarily for women, although men will find it valuable too. It can connect us with the power of the "shadow" by reconnecting us with one of the most powerful "shadow" figures in Western magic: Morgain.

As with so many legendary, romantic individuals, there are conflicting versions about who or what Morgain was and is. The twelfth-century historian and chronicler Geoffrey of Monmouth wrote that "her beauty surpasses that of her nine sisters. Her name is Morgain, and she has learned the uses of all plants in curing the ills of the body. She knows, too, the art of changing her shape, of flying through the air . . . she had taught astrology to her sisters."

Morgain was a healer, a shapechanger, a Witch. Early accounts tell us she was an Old Goddess of Sovereignty, the Mistress and Ruler of Avalon, the High Priestess of the Old Celtic Religion. She was Arthur's half sister and may have been taught magic and astronomy by Merlin. Some thought she was "a haughty Faerie" because she was a symbol of female rebellion against male authority. When angry, Morgain was difficult to please or appease; at other times she could be sweet, gentle, and good-natured. She was also described as the "warmest and most sensual woman in all Britain."

Morgain was an enigma to her political and religious adversaries. Christian scribes turned her into a demon, most likely because of her role as priestess in the Old Religion, which they were trying to discredit in their attempts to Christianize the power structure of Britain. She, however, valiantly defended the Faerie faith and the ancient Druidic practices, finding her most loyal supporters among the plain folk and simple peasantry of the countryside. She defied the accusations of Christian monks and missionaries that she was a harlot.

In time, Morgain's ability, or her desire, to pass "between the worlds" was undermined, and today her power resides mainly in the Otherworld. Now we must go to her and enter her world, and bring her back into ours. We encourage every magic-worker and lover to invoke her assistance and welcome her into our magic circles. Already many Witches use Morgain as a Craft name and practice magic for her. She can be a powerful ally for women reclaiming those powers of femininity that only surface in "bad" dreams at night, women seeking reassurance that it is all right to exercise their Faerie power, to be able to cross between the worlds.

Meditation: In a cauldron or any fired pot burn incense. Darken the room or wait till night. Light a black candle to represent the hidden, rebellious power of Morgain's magic. Dress like Morgain if you wish: wear chain mail bracelets or headpiece, wear a crown with a silver crescent moon, carry a sword or dagger in your belt. Go into alpha, and burn incense so that the smoke is strong and steady. Gaze into it deeply and smell its aromatic power to change the character of a room or chamber. After several minutes you will feel Morgain's presence in the room with you, perhaps beside you, or within you. She, too, gazes into the smoke. She, too, smells its sweet perfume.

Then say to yourself: "I am the Witch who stands beneath the moon. I am the roar of the Ocean. I am the Mistress of Sovereignty. I am the rain in the grass. I am the stars wheeling overhead. I am the seer of fortunes. I am a warrior strong with a sword. I am the sharp point of a sword. I am the gypsy mother, heavy with milk. I am a woman strong in the thighs. I am a woman who chooses her lovers. I teach the mysteries of the bed. I am the pleasure of coupling bodies. I am the joy of orgasm. I am the Witch who understands the power of love. I am Morgain. I have been alive forever. There is nothing in which I have not been."

You may add your own invocations of power, or eliminate or restate them so they feel right for you. Also, don't hesitate to repeat any invocation that has particular power or resonance for you, or repeat it with slight variations. Repetition creates the chant that leads into trance.

At some point you will enter a trancelike state, its intensity depending on your ability to alter consciousness. At this point your identification with Morgain will not be just in your imagination. In alpha, we can shapechange into Morgain's consciousness. At that point, you will not have to consciously *imagine* that you are the Mistress of Magic. On a psychic level, you are. And you *know* that you are.

When you have become Morgain, spend as much time as you wish, or as long as you are able to sustain the altered mood, tending the cauldron, adding incense, and gazing into and beyond the billows of smoke. Scry the smoke, watching for change and information. Ask your questions, state your intentions, seek your wisdom. Or do nothing at all, but sit and watch and learn what you can from being Morgain.

When the mood seems to shift and your consciousness is returning to your ordinary self, end the trance by stating just one or two of the invocative lines that seem appropriate at the moment, and finish with the last two lines: "I have been alive forever. There is nothing in which I have not been."

The Blade and the Chalice

In almost every culture, a cup, chalice, pot, bowl, cauldron, or basket is a feminine symbol: round, protective, inward, unifying, combining and synthesizing its contents, doing what it does by just being, allowing change to occur from within. The cup or chalice is a container, like the mother who contains the child in her womb and the milk to nurse the child in her rounded breasts. Water, another feminine element, is the original source of all life. The Great Sea Mother, from which mammals emerged many millennia ago, is the macrocosm of every mother nurturing an unborn life in the waters of her womb. It is not strange, therefore, that the earliest peoples saw in the cup or cauldron a shape and a purpose that reflect the Great Mother of All Living Things. Some anthropologists suggest the first human tools were not weapons but bowls or curved containers for scooping up and carrying water and for softening food for babies.

The blade is a masculine symbol: linear, penetrating, separating, forceful, targeted outside itself. In some circles today it is associated almost exclusively with war, violence, and the threat of death. It has an obvious phallic shape and has been the primary tool in man's historic role as hunter and warrior.

In the most simplistic view, the blade opposes the cup. The cup gives life. The blade takes life. The former is positive; the latter, negative. From a pagan perspective, it is not that simple. Giving and taking life are complementary roles, both part of the Great Wheel of Nature. Death is not a punishment for sin (as it is in the Christian worldview), but a natural event in the ongoing cycle of birth–death–rebirth. Death is a doorway into the Otherworld. The male principle, therefore, is not less noble than the female, for only by hunting and harvesting food can human life be sustained. It is a cosmic paradox, but death breeds life, and in death are the seeds of new life. Only when the taking of life is wanton, unnecessary, or cruel and sadistic does it deserve condemnation.

The Celts (as we might suspect) did not view cauldrons and swords as exclusively female and male. Many male heroes owned cauldrons, just as women warriors were experts in swordcraft. The Dagda, the primary Father God of the Tuatha Dē Danaan, had a cauldron of abundance, a kind of cornucopia, which satisfied everyone who came to it. The Dagda's cauldron also had the ability to heal. Bran the Blessed, a king of Britain, had a cauldron into which slain warriors were put to be reborn. His cauldron refused to "boil the food of a coward." In his early life, Arthur and his youthful companions stole a cauldron from the King of the Underworld, a feat paralleled by the Irish hero Cuchulainn, who stole a cauldron from the Irish Sea God

Manannan mac Lir. The boy Gwion, who later was reborn as the great Welsh poet Taliesin, was assigned to stir Cerridwen's cauldron, and when he licked a few drops of the mystical brew from his fingers, he acquired all wisdom and knowledge. In Scandinavian lore, Hymir, the sea giant, owned a magic cauldron. In Arthurian lore, women are the bearers of the Grail, but men are its guardians and the ones who quest after it. And so it goes: the shining dance of masculinity and feminity, blades and cauldrons, men and women.

Celtic customs, once again, confirm a great psychological truth about the human psyche. Human consciousness (the primary stuff of magic) is bisexual. Men have magic cauldrons or cups, and some die for them. Women are warriors, owning and brandishing swords and knives with the greatest skill. As a Witch I use a sword to initiate my students into the Craft in a dubbing ceremony very similar to the old ritual that dubbed someone a knight. As we have seen, Celtic women taught the martial arts to young men. King Arthur himself received his sword, Excalibur, from the Lady of the Lake, a magical weapon forged by Priestesses of the Goddess on the Isle of Avalon. When his reign ended, he was honor bound to return it to the Lady and the realm of feminine consciousness from which it came. Peredur, one of the Grail knights, received his arms and training from the Nine Witches of Gloucester. And so, we see once again the complementary powers of masculine and feminine.

Understanding how these feminine and masculine symbols "switch gender," so to speak, in myth and folklore inspires us to take them seriously as worthy images for love magic. Not only are they powerful concepts for focusing attention and activating our Inner Partners, but the blade and the cup demonstrate in ritual the union of the male and female at the heart of hetero-sexual relationships.

Ritual: This ritual requires some kind of blade and cup. Witches may want to use their athames, chalices, or cauldrons. Non-Witches could use a hunting knife, a wine goblet, a ce-ramic bowl, or wooden cup. Prepare the knife by wiping it clean of any dirt or oil. Fill the cup with wine, apple juice, or springwater. Cast a circle and go into alpha.

Sit for a few moments meditating on the Grail story: A young knight seeking the Grail passes through a dry, arid Wasteland and comes upon an old man fishing. The fisherman is actually the Grail King and is suffering from a lance wound in his loins. The wound will not heal, and so the King has given up hunting and warfare, and spends his time fishing. The King's realm is suffering from a blight, pestilence, or drought mysteri-ously connected to his wound. (Some legends point out that all the wells have dried up and the Maidens of the Wells have vanished.) The King invites the young knight to a banquet at the castle where the knight sees a procession of beautiful women carrying precious objects into the banquet hall. Here he sees the Grail and a Lance dripping blood. He wants to ask what these wondrous things mean, but he has been taught not to be nosy or curious and to keep his thoughts to himself. The next morning when he awakes, the castle, the King, the women, the Grail, and the Lance have disappeared. Later he learns that had he asked about the Grail and the Lance, the King would have been healed and the land would have been restored.

Like most mythic tales, this story contains many themes: courage and cowardice, authority and submission, health and disease, land stewardship, age and youth, male and female pow-ers. Each time you do this meditation, choose some aspect or set of polarities to focus on so that the tale becomes rich and meaningful for you. (You might also read up on the Grail legend and discover the many variations that have come down to us.)

After reflecting on the story of the Grail and the Lance, take the chalice in both hands, hold it up, and speak an invocation to honor its energy. A suggestion: "I praise the Cup as a container of life, as a giver of life, as the Great Mother upon whom all living things depend. I honor the Lady of the Cup and the blessings she bestows."

Then place the cup back down and pick up the knife in both hands, holding it up high in front of you, the blade pointed upward. Make an invocation, along the lines: "I praise the power of the Blade to change and separate, to send back life to the Great Mother from whom all life comes. I honor the Lord of the Hunt and the Spiritual Warrior and the strength and courage they bestow."

Then pick up the chalice in your left hand, and hold the blade in your right, pointed downward, directly over the cup. Raise them to eye level and ask the Grail questions the young knight failed to ask:

- ◆ "Whom does the Grail serve?"
- ◆ "Why does the Lance bleed?"
- ◆ "What do these Wonders mean?"

Next lower the point of the knife into the cup, and cut a pentacle (a five-pointed star within a circle) across the surface of the wine or water. Become aware of the roles played by both Blade and Chalice. Then remove the knife, shake whatever drops of liquid remain on the blade into the cup, and slowly, consciously drink the wine or water.

You have now internalized the mysteries of the Blade and the Chalice. Do this ritual whenever you feel a need to bring together the masculine and feminine aspects of your psyche. Couples can do this ritual together (see Chapter 8). The more obvious roles are for the woman to raise and invoke the cup, the man handles the blade. But in the Celtic spirit, you should reverse roles now and then, allowing these two powerful symbols to become part of each person's consciousness.

This is a powerful ritual for healing. The remarkable point of the Grail stories is that the mere asking of the Grail questions heals the king and restores the land. The answers do not seem to be important, and after many centuries of telling and retelling the story of the Grail, we still do not agree on what those answers are, or even if there are any answers. In fact, there is little agreement on what the Grail itself actually is. The questions themselves are haunting and bestow wisdom, understanding, and compassion on modern Grail seekers who ask them regularly and humbly.

Lovers: Star-Crossed or Star-Woven?

$\mathcal{L}$overs have always looked to the night skies, the phases of the moon, the journeys of the planets, and the position of the sun for guidance about the most important aspects in their lives. A troubled relationship is "star-crossed"; a happy, carefree affair is "written in the stars"; some marriages are thought to be "made in heaven." I married into a star-crossed love thirty years ago, and when it ended, I wrote this poem to the Goddess and wore a silver ring dedicated to her so that she would help me find a love that was more appropriate.

> *The blood flows and surges through*
> *my body, but the moon changes course,*
> *certain will my blood's course reverse.*
> *The fluid of the soul will be pressured*
> *to retract its way and yet find another.*

Oh, would that I could set the courses
of the stars and moon to a perfect
direction, my purpose would be clear
and the way easy to the Goddess.

In some concentric way the majestic procession of the galaxies parallels our journey through starlight and moonlight and through the ups and downs of human experience. The Goddess stays with us. The magic of the heart is illuminated by the planets and stars that witnessed our births and continue to journey with us around the rim of constellations over the course of our lives.

Human affairs are ever at the push and tug of celestial events. The moon governs our psychological balance. It pulls the tides, initiates a woman's menstrual flow, gently summons plants from the dark womb of earth, and when it is full, increases human births and, ironically, the number of reported crimes. In a like manner, the sun shines on and influences human activities. Without sufficient sunlight, especially during the winter months in northern latitudes, people suffer from seasonal affective disorder (SAD), and solar flares and sunspots correspond to disruptive events in human history, possibly because of the accompanying shifts in the positive and negative ions of the atmosphere (which influence moods and sense of well-being). The transit of planets across the sky and through the signs of the zodiac also brings change and transformation in human affairs.

In this chapter we will look at ways to draw the power of the stars into our magic. The chapter is divided into four parts. "Star Magic" explains how Witches use astrology in spells and magic. "Drawing Down Celestial Light" is a ritual to invoke the help of Merlin in your love-work. "Love Among the Stars" offers suggestions on how to use sun signs to enhance your relationship. "Love Among the Elements" contains ten spells for using the elements—air, fire, water, stone—to strengthen and bond two lovers.

STAR MAGIC

Witches use astrology in very specific ways for spells and rituals. Here are some basic principles to use in love spells. Monday (Moon), Tuesday (Mars), and Friday (Venus) are the best days of the week for love magic. Become acquainted with the movement and phases of the moon by consulting a lunar calendar. When the moon is a young, silver crescent, do spells for growth and new beginnings. Spells to increase love, bring love into your life, or attract a lover are most successful during a waxing moon or three hours before it is full. A waning moon is the time of the month for magic to remove obstacles in love and to neutralize problems in relationships. The dark of the moon is the most powerful time for spells to banish obstacles preventing you from growing in love and being a good partner and lover. Learn to be at home in all the phases of the moon because moonlight breathes romance, bestows hunches, and penetrates to the psychic marrow of your life.

Your sun sign fixes your most constant pattern or style of loving. Who, what, when, and where you love is seen most clearly in the sign where the sun resided when you were born. Sun signs are not inflexible conditions, however; they are tendencies and predispositions with room for growth and change. It is always possible to balance or temper the most negative aspects of our sun signs preventing us from enjoying life and becoming an easy partner to love and live with. Knowledge about your sun sign, as well as your lover's, is a useful guide for your mutual journey through life.

All the planets vibrate with their specific music, contributing to what medieval philosophers called "the music of the spheres." Spells in harmony with the most prominent planets in your life and your lover's life will be the most effective.

Venus, for example, rules sensuality, desire, passion, and erotic beauty. The music of Venus is a song of love, harmony, and sensual pleasure. As the Greek Goddess of Love, Aphrodite, says, "All acts of love and pleasure are mine," meaning they are sacred. Witchcraft is free from the guilt-ridden dogmas of some religions that claim the human body and sexuality are barriers to spiritual growth and signs of our downfall from a state of grace. For Witches, all sensual pleasures express the divine fecundity of the universe and the ecstatic joy we are meant to experience when we encounter the God and Goddess in ourselves and others.

I suggest you find a good astrologer, have your chart done, and then a comparative chart for your loved one to see if you are compatible. You can then request a double chart for you and your partner. Consult your astrologer when there are major changes in your relationship or once a year just to keep in touch with the stars and planets that govern your chart.

The Wheel of the Year—the sky and earth changes, patterns of weather, climatic changes, the procession of the seasons—all echo in our hearts and in the love we create with another person. Love is the experience of cosmic energy, it moves through us, like channels, reaching out to others. We owe it to ourselves and the ones we love to understand these movements of human emotion and celestial energies. In short, we should follow the stars because among them is our true home. We are star-people, wandering on this marvelous green planet, navigating our ships by the stars, looking for love and a way home. Ideally, love *is* the way home.

DRAWING DOWN CELESTIAL LIGHT

Merlin, that crafty wizard and stargazer of Arthurian times, asked for an observatory to be built with seventy doors and seventy windows for watching the night skies. In the twelfth-century account *Vita Merlini,* he says, "I will watch fire-breathing Phoebus and Venus and the stars gliding from the heavens by night, all of whom shall show me what is going to happen to the people of the kingdom." Tradition says that Merlin still watches over magical people and his star-filled wizardry continues to radiate through the sacred forests of Britain. Whenever I travel to England I always bring back oak leaves, acorns, and branches that have accumulated centuries of starlight, the same repositories of celestial lore Merlin uses to divine what will come and what has been.

Starlight shines on everyone, of course, and all of us can collect its radiance from the oaks and apple trees wherever we live and use it in our magic. At the top of the hill behind Tom's house is a large orchard where he collects oak and apple wood for sacred fires. When you look deeply into the flames, you can sometimes see the light from the stars. While oak and apple have special significance in traditional Celtic magic, any tree, leaf, or fruit contains star magic because every tree unites earth and heaven. Each tree's roots penetrate deep into the earth's mysteries, and its branches mirror the root-spread up into the sky where the ever-changing, starry Wheel of the Year calls forth bud, leaf, flower, fruit, harvest, death, and always another time of new budding.

Here is a ritual to draw down celestial light to illuminate
your love life:

Two nights before the full moon, walk through a wooded
place, and go to an oak. Gather a few fallen leaves and acorns,
requesting Merlin's blessing from his home inside the oak
where legend says the old shapeshifter waits until people wisen
up and ask him once more for his help. You are now doing that.
He will respond.

Take a large quartz crystal, wash it in sea salt, and leave it in
the window or outdoors overnight to gather the light of the
waxing moon and the radiance of the season's stars. In the
morning, charge the crystal and the oak leaves and acorns,
specifically drawing in Merlin's power. (Be careful about leaving
powerful crystals on the windowsill in the morning; some have
concentrated the sunlight on the wooden sill and caused fires.)
Visualize him inside the crystal, even as he is in the oak and all
its leaves and nuts. Feel his presence, especially the star-and-
planet-power woven into his magical robes. Raise a mist, the
dragon's breath, around you, remembering the mists of England
that bathe oak, leaf, hill, and lake. Every mist holds the ancient
memory of magic, of a time when people were more keenly
aware of the mystery of how all things are connected, interlaced, and interwoven like a Celtic knot. Hold that memory
now as you charge these sacred objects.

In the hour before the moon is full, bring to a wooded place
or a window where the moon shines, the crystal, three leaves,
and three acorns, a golden harp (or a picture of a harp), a piece
of meteor or a star-map. Light three candles, silver, blue,
and pink. Carve one of the following three words onto each
candle: *lover, kind, true.* Then on a piece of paper write this
spell:

> *A lover, kind and true,*
> *Will come to me*
> *When this spell comes due.*

Touch the paper with the crystal. Leave the spell in a special place covered by the leaves and acorns. Keep the crystal especially for love magic, and invoke Merlin whenever you use it.

LOVE AMONG THE STARS

People often come to me with questions like "I'm in love with a Virgo. How should I treat her?" or "I met a gorgeous man on the commuter train who says he's a Pisces. How can I turn him on?" Although this is not a book on astrology, I have put together some general characteristics of each sun sign, which can be used to oil the wheels of most relationships. My coven uses the herbs, oils, colors, and jewelry associated with the various signs to influence bosses, supervisors, teachers, neighbors, or family members. They are not just for love spells. These are the objects that vibrate with each person's sun-sign energy. Wear, carry, or use them, and you may appear more compatible to the person you are trying to influence. Charge them in a magic circle or touch them with love potion, and they become magical tools with even more influence.

 ARIES MAN (*March 21—April 19*)

The Aries man is active, explosive, adventurous, and self-disciplined. Ruled by the planet Mars, Aries men do not like to be dominated or supervised. They want to call the shots. They generally like partners who can be sexy and intelligent at the same time. I remember a woman who tried to attract an Aries man with every trick she knew. She forgot the major trick: Let him make the first move! Aries men are seductive and like to take the lead in relationships, especially early on. Aries men like their would-be lovers to declare their feelings, but I think it is best to hold yourself back even if you are passionately in love with him. Take things slowly. They like mates who share their interests. As fire signs, Aries men remind me of the Sun Gods: powerful, intelligent, clear-minded. They also exhibit considerable psychic powers and, like the Sun Gods, are protective of the ones they love.

The following items have special appeal to Aries men: white, red, or blue clothing; gold jewelry. Use these ingredients in spells: herbs—ginger, nettle, peppercorns; stones—hematite, ruby, garnet, diamond, lava; oils—cassia, cinnamon, calamus, geranium, patchouli.

 TAURUS MAN (*April 20—May 20*)

A bull-like man, Taurus can be both paternal and maternal toward someone. He is always protective. As an earth sign, he loves the hearth and home. Taurus usually wants marriage, but before he settles down, he can be stubbornly independent and motivated only by work or career. Most Taureans are well groomed and well dressed. Ruled by the planet Venus, they fall for women who also dress well and have the characteristics of the Love Goddess. They prefer their mates to be well educated and well informed, and able to hold up their end of a conversation about business and finances. A Taurean appreciates nurturing lovers who take an interest in his well-being. Taureans are very straightforward and usually don't like surprises.

The following items have a special appeal to Taureans: rose, green, or copper-colored clothing; silver or copper jewelry. Use these ingredients in spells and rituals: stones—malachite, rose quartz; oils—lily of the valley, lotus; herbs—patchouli, apple blossom.

♊ GEMINI MAN (*May 21—June 20*)

Geminis are air signs. Like the wind and weather, they can be restless and unpredictable. Ruled by the planet Mercury, Geminis thrive on change and are comfortable in changeable situations. All the Gemini men I know have a quick wit, a clever tongue, and a good sense of repartee, making them good lecturers and teachers, or terrific salesmen. A Gemini's personality, like his sign, is dual. People in love with Gemini often complain that it is as if their lovers had split personalities. Gemini men are similar to Trickster Gods, who can be quick-change artists. They usually love to be around lots of people and can be the life of a party.

The following items have a special appeal to a Gemini: gray, white, yellow, or black clothing; silver, platinum, or copper jewelry. Use these ingredients in spells and rituals: oils—patchouli, rose; stones—turquoise, coral, aventurine; herbs—lavender, horehound, dill, scullcap, cinquefoil.

69 CANCERIAN MAN (*June 21—July 22*)

Cancerian men can be shy and complain a lot. It all depends on the moon's influence. Always keep a moon calendar close at hand, and keep a log of his moods correlated to the moon's phases. You'll be able to predict his ups and downs much better. Often Cancerians will brood and turn sullen over small remarks. But try not to blame them. They are a water sign, and at the mercy of the moon. Be patient. Sometimes Cancerians are extremely quiet and uncommunicative. At other times they are quite witty and fun to be around. The Cancerian men I have known over the years could all be stand-up comedians if they put their minds to it. Unfortunately, they are not always the type who gets stagestruck. Like the Sea Gods that influence them, they can be isolated individuals, preferring to spend time in their own hideaways where they will not have to meet strangers. A shy Cancerian will never confide in a stranger, so approach him in a gentle manner, no matter what kind of mood he is in.

The following items have special appeal to Cancerian men: light blue, green, or lavender clothing; silver or gold jewelry. Use these ingredients in spells and rituals: oils—jasmine, rose, sweet pea, cerridwen oil; stones—clear quartz, moonstone; herbs—mushrooms, watercress, water lily.

♌ LEO MAN (*July 23—August 22*)

Leo is always king. He's number one. Extremely ambitious, he loves the limelight, and will make loud speeches if he has an audience. A fixed fire sign, a Leo can be stubborn and demanding. He likes and needs lots of attention, like the Sun Gods who influence him. If you want a Leo, you must go to him, meet him on his turf, and look like his equivalent: the height of fashion, well groomed, regal, at your best. Leos can be very narcissistic, really taken with themselves, and they often expect their partners to be ornaments that reflect their luster. I remember a woman interested in a Leo man who never got to first base with him. It turned out her style of dressing was just too casual for him ("sloppy" is the way he perceived it). When she scaled up her wardrobe to reflect his, he suddenly saw her in a different light. A Leo appreciates directness and a no-nonsense approach.

The following have special appeal to Leos: clothing in the primary colors; gold jewelry. Use these ingredients in spells and rituals: oils—love potion, olive, saffron, storax; stones—garnet, yellow topaz, cat's eye; herbs—chamomile, frankincense, galougal, High Joan, marigold.

♍ VIRGO MAN (*August 22—September 22*)

Virgos try to be perfectionists. They have strong views of how things should be and are very critical of themselves and others. They are hard to please (some can never be pleased). They are often in search of the perfect world. Your conversation and behavior must make sense to him if he is to take you seriously. Virgos are artistic and sensitive, but not always romantic. A Virgo takes his time getting to know someone new. Virgos like seemingly weak and disorganized partners, and I have known a lot of them who see themselves as Apollos coming to rescue those in trouble. They themselves often have strong needs, especially for companionship on all levels. They can be very demanding emotionally. Most of the women I have counseled who fell in love with Virgo men had real problems getting them to settle down, since Virgo is the sign of the bachelor. Even though Virgo is an earth sign, and Virgo men have a strong desire for hearth, home, and creature comforts, a typical Virgo male may not feel good about marriage. Perhaps it is the influence of the planet Mercury that keeps him changing his mind about getting married. Virgos don't like to spend money and have a natural talent for saving and investing.

The following items have special appeal to Virgos: light blue, white, gray, black, or brown clothing; gold and platinum jewelry. Use these ingredients in spells and rituals: oils—neroli, sandalwood, and any oil with a fresh, soapy fragrance; stones— quartz, lodestone, sapphire; herbs—tea, sassafras, savory, parsley, mace, mandrake.

⚏ LIBRA MAN (*September 23—October 22*)

A Libra is always seeking balance in his life, although some of them are not very good at maintaining the balance. Libra is the sign of the scales and really does tend to weigh every little incident and emotion in life. Libra men love long-lasting relationships. They are good candidates for marriage. But when the scales tip and their lives become unbalanced, they can easily fall in love with whoever is nearest and kindest to them. Women involved with Libras frequently complain that their men often go after other women who are already taken. Libras are ruled by the planet Venus and are strong air signs. A Libra man can be very persuasive and charming. He likes to solve problems and will be glad to help you with yours. Tell him about your troubles or needs. Libras like lots of admiration and attention. The more Libras feel involved in your life, the closer they feel to you.

The following items have special appeal to Libras: green, copper, rose, pink, or brown clothing; silver or gold jewelry. Use these ingredients in spells and rituals: oils—verbena, violet, apple blossom, love potion, rose; herbs—yarrow, clover, burdock, bergamot, laurel; stones—emerald, malachite, rose quartz.

♏ SCORPIO MAN (*October 23—November 21*)

A Scorpio works and lives passionately and has deep-seated feelings. He needs a cause: a religion, political party, a way of life, or a person to love and care for. Like the water sign he is, a Scorpio can drown others by dominating them. Scorpios like to be leaders. A Scorpio man wants a passionate romance but one that he can manipulate, which he often does by his sexual prowess. If outrageously jealous, he will need a partner who can lighten up his moods and absolutely not accept his jealous behavior. I have seen many jealous Scorpio males become very abusive. It can begin with sarcasm and cutting words. But in spite of these negative traits, Scorpios are very creative and extremely faithful once they have committed themselves in relationships. Ruled by the distant planet Pluto, typical Scorpios are secretive and attracted to others who love secrets and have mysterious ways about them. Magic both intrigues and frightens them. I knew a typical Scorpio who was always afraid I was going to discover his secrets by my psychic abilities. He was always uncomfortable around me.

The following items have special appeal to Scorpios: red, black, or white clothing; gold, silver, or platinum jewelry. Use these ingredients in spells and rituals: oils—dragon's blood, love potion, cerridwen oil; herbs—cherriel, cohosh, dogwood, dwarf elder, foxglove; stones—obsidian, ruby, agate, amber.

 SAGITTARIUS MAN (*November 22—December 21*)

Like their fire element, Sagittarius men are always active, often outdoors, frequently engaged in sports, which they like to play with their mates. They like challenges and even indoor games like cards and Scrabble. They tend to be youthful and playful, putting their names or initials in fresh cement or touching signs that say DO NOT TOUCH. They like their freedom and can't be pigeonholed. Sagittarius men frequently complain to me that their partners are always trying to put a leash on them. When they think that is what is happening, they run! A Sagittarius loves novelty, likes to travel, enjoys a new joke or a new idea. Even though he may play the little boy, he needs a lover, not a parent. Sagittarians are usually successful with money. Their ruling planet, Jupiter, helps them win and find good careers. Sagittarians, male and female, often want the lover that just got away or the one they can't have. If your Sagittarian talks about his last love, be understanding, not jealous, and you will win his confidence and devotion.

The following items have special appeal for Sagittarians: royal blue, turquoise, or purple clothing; gold or pewter jewelry. Use these ingredients in spells and rituals: oils—cinnamon, jasmine, money oil, magnolia, myrrh, hyacinth; herbs— sumac, spinach, sandalwood, rose hips; stones—lapis lazuli, amethyst, jasper.

♑ CAPRICORN MAN *(December 22—January 19)*

Young Capricorn boys argue with their parents about everything and often keep this trait into adult life, but their loyalty to family and loved ones is long-lasting. Capricorns are clever and ambitious, making good executives and often running their own businesses. Ruled by the planet Saturn, a Capricorn tends to be obsessive and compulsive about certain things, such as career and relationships, and will express his anxieties to you. Typical Capricorns often have money as a primary goal, but they can be generous and show they love you by providing you with gifts and material things. They like to show they really care for you by deeds, and may not come right out and say, "I love you." A Capricorn can be a pack rat and save everything he has ever owned, both for himself and for you. He hates to lose things, but he does: money, keys, jewelry. Capricorns like to take pride in their mates, so show your best side. Like the God

Pan, he is an earthy lover, open to sexual adventures. When women tell me their partners are always proposing new and unusual ways to make love, I often suspect they are Capricorns, ruled by the Goat-footed God. Capricorns are charming, but their sense of humor borders on the sarcastic. They greatly fear death and they love life.

The following items have special appeal to Capricorns: red, black, burgundy, or purple clothing; gold, platinum, silver, and pewter jewelry. Use these ingredients in rituals and spells: oils —love oil, patchouli, bergamot, money oil; herbs—datura flower, patchouli, tobacco, Solomon's seal, shepherd's purse, poppy, pomegranate, ivy; stones—onyx, jet diamond.

≈≈ AQUARIUS MAN (*January 20—February 18*)

Ruled by the planet Uranus, Aquarians are always concerned about the world's problems but may be blind to the needs of their own families and loved ones. An Aquarian's family may be the last to get his attention, especially if he has already provided them with food, shelter, and clothing. Then he will be looking for bigger issues. In spite of Aquarians' outside concerns, they are usually up for a sexual romp and are always looking for new ways to do everything, including making love. The Aquarian man hates mundane topics and petty details, so don't bother him with them. Aquarians' attention spans are short, like children's. Just when you think you have his attention, he is usually thinking about something else. But Aquarians like to play, usually have a good sense of humor, and make good vacation partners. They are not turned on by physical beauty and charm alone, but need intellectual stimulation. Like the Celtic God Lug, they are often good at many things and are interested in their partners' minds as well as their bodies. Love of money lures Aquarians to go after wealthy women or mates who look like they could earn a lot or run their own businesses.

The following items have special appeal to Aquarians: purple, lavender, pink, or black clothing; gold or silver jewelry. Use these ingredients in spells and rituals: oils—cinnamon, clove, coffee; herbs—allspice, chicory, nutmeg, unicorn root, mandrake; stones—smoky quartz, amethyst, chalcedony.

♓ PISCES MAN (*February 19—March 20*)

A water sign, ruled by the planet Neptune, Pisces males may seem wishy-washy on the surface, but underneath they are quite solid. A Pisces can be very charming, witty, and flirtatious. I think Pisces men make the best lovers in the zodiac. But a Pisces male needs a lot of romantic attention, so bring him flowers and invite him to candle-lit dinners. I have never known a Pisces man who didn't crave poetry, music, romantic movies, and beauty in all forms. Pisces can be very nurturing and sympathetic. However, if things go wrong, Pisces quickly lose all these fine qualities. Some Pisces can be very self-centered and successful, their work or career always coming first. A Pisces needs to stand on his own two feet, however, so don't make him too dependent on you. Remember that a Pisces man needs a lot of encouragement and tender loving care. Often like a Sea God, he knows or suspects that he has deep psychic abilities.

The following items have special appeal to Pisces men: light green, orchid, blue, white, lavender, or orchid clothing; silver, gold, or pewter jewelry. Use these ingredients in spells and rituals: oils—apricot, lemon, lotus, opium, neroli; herbs—passion flower, peach, pear, poppy seed, wisteria, adam and eve root; stones—aquamarine, coral, seashells, clear quartz.

♈ ARIES WOMAN (*March 21—April 19*)

An Aries woman is very sociable, adventurous, enthusiastic, with a healthy touch of curiosity. A restless person typical of fire signs, she needs variety and spontaneity in her life. Aries women are attracted to active, on-the-go males. An Aries woman likes to be chased, so call her every day and make sure you stay on the scene. Most Aries women I have known never hesitate to say what's on their minds even if you don't want to hear it. Being outspoken, she will usually answer questions in an upfront, honest way. She is very giving, hospitable, and eager to please. Most are good cooks and proud of their homes. Aries's preferences in men lean toward a mixed type: rugged, deep voice, but with a touch of glamor. Aries women have a soft spot in their hearts for underdogs. A lot of Aries women appear to be fragile, but their birthstone is the tough diamond, and because they are ruled by the planet Mars, their metal is iron. I like to think of them as having the woman-warrior energy of the Amazons or of the Celtic warrior-Witch, Scathach. Aries women are tough, sexy, and exciting.

The following items have special appeal to Aries: white, blue, red, or black clothing; silver, gold, steel, or iron jewelry.

Use these ingredients in spells and rituals: oils—hyssop, pine, love oil, Cerridwen oil; herbs—nettle, marjoram, pepper, cumin, coriander; stones—hematite, pyrite, agate, ruby, garnet, diamond, rhodochrosite.

 ## TAURUS WOMAN (*April 20—May 20*)

Taurean women are unabashed about flirting with their eyes and chasing the lovers they are after. In sexual situations they may be shy about making the first move, but once begun they show a lot of initiative. Being a Hearth Goddess type, a Taurus woman wants her home to be a warm, loving place. She loves good food and great wines, whether at a four-star restaurant or as home-cooking. A Taurus woman can be lured by a strong whiff of love potion, the scent of freshly washed hair, burning leaves, and fresh baked bread. She usually has a green thumb and can grow anything from indoor plants to bank accounts. Like the Bull, she can be very fixed in her ways, and easily becomes one-track-minded when involved with a person or a pet project. One of my male clients got on the bad side of his Taurean lover and discovered to his dismay that she had a gossipy tongue and went to great lengths to get even with him. This seems typical of Taurean women who feel they have been wronged. On the social side, a Taurus likes art exhibits, plays, and concerts. Taurean women usually have a good sense of humor and enjoy comedy.

The following items have special appeal to Taureans: pink, green, brown, or beige clothing; gold or copper jewelry. Use these ingredients in spells and rituals: oils—lemon verbena, love potion, Cerridwen oil, rose, neroli, gardenia; herbs—apple blossom, birch, blackberry, catnip, daisies, heather; stones—emerald, beryl, diamond.

♊ GEMINI WOMAN (*May 21—June 20*)

A Gemini woman is several women all rolled into one. I encourage men who want change and spice in their lives to look for a Gemini lover. Like a Goddess of the Hunt, she has a great need for change of pace in all areas of her life. Ruled by the planet Mercury and being influenced by the element of air, a Gemini can be very changeable. A Gemini woman is drawn to people who have unusual careers, personalities, or offbeat lifestyles. She may act as if flowers, cards, and candy don't impress her, but your efforts to please her do not go unnoticed. Intellectually, she is usually well informed and interested in many fields. Gemini women are often perpetual students. Geminis seem split over their need for domesticity. They hate housework, but are very practical around the house. A Gemini would rather leave the cooking up to someone else, so invite her over for meals or out to dinner often. Geminis are born flirts, sometimes to the point of embarrassment, and can be extremely sexy.

The following items have special appeal to Gemini: gray, orange, blue, or lavender clothing; silver, pewter, or platinum jewelry. Use these ingredients in spells and rituals: oils—sandalwood, jasmine, rose, frankincense; herbs—bittersweet, caraway, cedar, honeysuckle, lavender, valerian; stones—agate, opal, carnelian, sardonyx, rutilated quartz, black tourmaline, mica.

CANCERIAN WOMAN (*June 21—July 22*)

A Cancerian woman can be naturally shy and very moody, but her come-on is often strong and romantic. However, don't come on too strong with her. Soften your approach and be gently and sweetly persistent. She is a water sign, ruled by the moon, so her moods can swing from high to low in quick succession. Cancerian females have a nesting personality. They will want to make a home and feed you because for them the home is a magic space where they can be very creative and sexy. In general Cancerians are sympathetic and good sounding boards for their partners. Like the Goddesses of Crafts that influence them, they have great artistic ability whether it be music and painting or horsemanship and comedy. A Cancerian-woman can dress like a queen or a punk rocker, given the right occasion. She likes a partner who looks healthy and physically fit.

The following items have special appeal to Cancerians: black, purple, light blue, silver, or gray clothing; silver, gold, or platinum jewelry. Use these ingredients in spells and rituals: oils—sandalwood, jasmine, Cerridwen oil, frankincense, myrrh; herbs—wild rose, coriander, star anise, water lily, moonwort, orris root; stones—moonstone, star sapphire, clear quartz, pearl, seashells.

♌ LEO WOMAN (*July 23—August 22*)

A Leo woman loves to play the queen and be the center of attention with lots of men flocking around her. A Leo wants to be number one and the *only* one in your life. And she needs constant reassurance about this. Usually expensive gifts (or a bouquet of wildflowers if you're short on money) will make the point. Give her lots of gifts. Like the Goddess Hera, she can be demanding and forceful, but in a sweet, self-assured way. Leos like to climb socially, so they gravitate toward rich and powerful people who look as if they're on the way up. A Leo has the clothing and grooming for the glamorous life, and if you are into that she is just the right woman to have on your arm. A passionate sign, she can also become extremely possessive. Like the lioness herself, she can have deadly claws, even though she has just used them to scratch your itching back! She can be a tiger in the bedroom (her element is fire) or a kitten on the couch. Leos have a compassionate side and are deeply touched by people in unfortunate situations.

The following items have special appeal to Leos: yellow, orange, red, or gold clothing; gold jewelry. Use these ingredients in spells and rituals: oils—frankincense, lovage, heliotrope, bayberry, almond; herbs—acorns, aloes, angelica, chamomile, eyebright, saffron, storax; stones—carnelian, peridot, sardonyx, topaz, cat's-eye.

♍ VIRGO WOMAN (*August 23—September 22*)

Virgo women are very critical of themselves and others. With their Athena-like personalities, they are easily turned on by intellect and a quick wit. A Virgo likes academic men, but any type of clever mind will always win her over. In her view, "smarts" are more important than "looks." She has psychic power to create perfect manifestations of her thoughts, and she usually has images in her mind of exactly what she wants and she often gets it. She desires the best in everything; she looks for perfection and expects it in her mates. Sadly, I know a lot of Virgo women who are extremely disappointed by reality! They fall in the trap of longing for someone else's partner and imagining that he is better in some way than their own. If you are the jealous type, this trait could drive you crazy! Also, don't take it too personally if a Virgo woman forgets to call you back once a relationship has begun. Be aggressive and keep after her. Virgos are spontaneous and mysterious, and they like surprises with a touch of romance and mystery.

The following items have special appeal to Virgos: blue, black, silver, or pink clothing; platinum and gold jewelry. Use these ingredients in spells and rituals: oils—clove, love potion, lavender; herbs—maidenhair, allspice, ginseng, mandrake, and unicorn root; stones—fire opal, clear quartz crystal, and rutilated quartz.

⚖ LIBRA WOMAN (*September 23—October 22*)

As a love partner, a Libra woman knows how to fulfill a man's dreams. She is Venus incarnate. She will always want to be part of what you are doing but not in a clinging way. As a rule, Libras do not like to go to noisy, confusing, distracting places. But they love music, arts, and design, so you might take a Libra (or meet one) in a quiet art gallery or at a low-keyed concert. Libras have trouble making up their minds and often go after someone because they admire the way that person lives his life or the choices he has made about his home or career. Some Libra women are attracted to men who will help them make decisions. It's not uncommon for Libras to get into love triangles, either because they have two lovers and can't give one up, or because they go after someone else's lover. Libras tend to find something they like in most people. Often men involved with Libras will tell me they fib and lie too much, but what you must remember is that it is not always malicious. A Libra will not always tell the exact truth because she likes to repress, ignore, or cover up things she doesn't like. Libras tend toward stable home lives and enjoy their houses, yards, apartments.

The following items have special appeal to Libras: beige, brown, rust, or green clothing; silver or copper jewelry. Use these ingredients in spells and rituals: oils—apple blossom, love potion, rose geranium, heather; herbs—hibiscus, kava, kava lemon, balin, strawberry, tansy; stones—beryl, emerald, rose quartz, malachite.

♏ SCORPIO WOMAN (*October 23—November 21*)

Scorpio women never seem to fall in the middle: they are either ladylike all the way or there is nothing ladylike about them. It seems to me that they embody the most dominant and alluring traits of all the Goddesses, and so they come on pretty strong and sexy. A water sign, Scorpios can fluctuate radically, and the influence of the planet Pluto can put them in dark, remote moods. Scorpio women have very set ideas about how they should lead their lives and how things should be done. Like Cerridwen pursuing Gwion for having crossed her, a Scorpio woman will hunt you down if you displease her. If they have not developed a satisfying way of life, Scorpio females can be very depressed and suspicious about almost everything in their lives, especially their mates. Almost every Scorpio female I know has the potential to be a very effective leader. They tend to be very passionate about almost everything they take an interest in. If you are trying to get to know a Scorpio, it is best to talk to her about her interests rather than yours, until you get a relationship going. Ask her about her philosophy of life; she has usually given it quite a bit of thought.

The following items have special appeal to Scorpios: red, black, or white clothing; gold and silver jewelry. Use these ingredients in spells and rituals: oils—love potion, dragon's blood, musk, patchouli; herbs—clathos, damiana, foxglove, hops, wheat; stones—obsidian, clear quartz, black tourmaline.

✗ SAGITTARIUS WOMAN (*November 22—December 21*)

Sagittarian women, like the Goddess of the Hunt, Diana, are active, youthful, sports-minded, always on the go. You might meet them on the ski slopes or tennis court, or at a comedy club. They prefer exciting, adventurous, athletic, outdoor dates rather than the candy-and-flowers approach. These gentler, romantic ploys tend not to impress them. They are attracted to light, fun-loving men. A Sagittarian is usually very direct in her approach (her sign is the Archer), and more apt to want to meet you if she feels some spark between the two of you. A lot of the Sagittarian women I know are romantic and psychic enough to discover in their lovers some connection with past lives. Because of her sense of humor, she might present herself in a joking, jovial way, but most Sagittarian women have big egos and hate to be ignored. Refer to her as "your friend," not "your girl" or "your woman." She does not want to be owned. Sagittarians are ruled by the planet Jupiter. With a temperament ruled by the element fire, they like to disagree with others, just to keep a sense of freedom, and they always want the last word, even in matters of love. They can keep you guessing. They like lovers who can look casual or flashy, men who change their appearances, such as the rugged outdoor look one day, urban punk the next.

The following items have special appeal to Sagittarians: royal blue, black, purple, turquoise, or pink clothing; pewter, silver, gold, or tin jewelry. Use these ingredients in spells and rituals: oils—cinnamon, cloves, jasmine, Cerridwen oil, money oil; herbs—henna, cinquefoil, tonka beans, dandelion, magnolia, milkweed, myrrh, thorn apple; stones—lapis lazuli, amethyst, chrysocolla, sapphire.

♑ CAPRICORN WOMAN (*December 22—January 19*)

A Capricorn woman is capable of ruling the world, and usually ends up ruling something: a family, her business, someone else's business. She gravitates toward power and powerful mates. Give her "power gifts" like money, saving bonds, expensive jewelry, antique coins. A Capricorn is impressed by success. She is attracted to strong, masculine partners, men who pump iron or exercise their brains. She needs brains as well as a body in a man. Capricorns are very psychic and can tell what you are all about in a glance. She can help you get in touch with your deeper, instinctual self. I've hardly known a Capricorn to mince words. If she doesn't like you, she will tell you immediately. She likes to be the center of attention. Because she is influenced by the element earth, she is drawn toward stability: a stable home, business, relationship. She can dress outrageously, possibly overdress. Even though she is naturally powerful and youthful appearing (even as she grows older), she needs reassurance.

The following items have special appeal to Capricorns: beige, gray, brown, or rust clothing; gold, silver, steel, iron, and pewter jewelry. Use these ingredients in spells and rituals: oils —musk, pansy, cherry, rose, apricot; herbs—apple blossom, bergamot, blackberry, burdock, cocoa, elder, goldenseal, holly, ivy, comfrey, aconite; stones—alexandrite, coal, geodes, kunzite.

≈≈ AQUARIUS WOMAN (*January 20—February 18*)

Aquarian women are the madcaps of the zodiac. Influenced by
the Faerie Goddesses, such as Una, they enjoy the unusual,
offbeat, strange, and they often get involved in bizarre escapades. With or without a college education, Aquarian women
will have studied a lot and picked up a lot of information about
many things. Ruled by Uranus and Saturn, an Aquarian loves to
play with abstract concepts even in the bedroom. Aquarian
women have short attention spans, however, so make your impression hard and fast. An Aquarian is an explorer, always looking for new and exciting ground to break. She has a playful
need for laughs and fun. She is turned on by witty, brainy
vibrations, mere physical charm won't work. She likes causes.
Aquarian women can be incurable romantics and very sweet,
once they get to know you. An Aquarian likes to lead the
parade.

The following items have special appeal to Aquarians: lavender, black, white, dazzling white clothing; platinum, silver,
or chrome jewelry. Use these ingredients in spells and rituals:
oils—apricot, lemon, opium, orange, peach, wisteria; herbs—
nutmeg, mandrake, chicory, burdock, ebony, rue; stones—
opal, rutilated quartz, clear quartz, jet.

)(PISCES WOMAN (*February 19—March 22*)

Pisces women are fun, nurturing, but very complex. They are
ruled by the planet Neptune and are born Witches. They need

to be held and cuddled, and often need others to make decisions for them. A water sign, they can display indecisiveness on many occasions. They are also very sensitive and may not tell you when you hurt them. Like the Celtic Goddess Blodewedd, she seems to be made of flowers, and the traditional love gifts will win her heart, as well as small animals like kittens, puppies, and fish. Love notes, knowing glances, and secret smiles turn her on because she so easily falls in love with love itself. When disappointed, however, she can drop a romance very quickly. Pisces tend to hold their anger inside. When a Pisces must act alone, she can be a real warrior. Pisces women have creative minds, in projects, business, relationships, and the bedroom.

The following items have special appeal to Pisces: light green, emerald, green, rose, lavender, black, white, gray, or purple clothing; platinum, pewter, tin, or gold jewelry. Use these ingredients in spells and rituals: oils—lotus, lily, patchouli, hyssop, lime, myrrh, tonka beans, jasmine; herbs—watercress, seaweed, grape leaves, lobelia, mugwort, narcissus, willow; stones—amethyst, sapphire, seashells, beryl, aquamarine, bloodstone, blue quartz.

LOVE AMONG THE ELEMENTS

Every human being is made up of earth, air, fire, and water. More than eighty percent of our bodies are water; our internal fire maintains a normal temperature of 98.6 degrees Fahrenheit; oxygen from the air in our lungs travels through our bloodstream to every cell in our bodies; and bones, flesh, teeth, hair, and nails are our solid, earthy substances. The four human temperaments, defined by Hippocrates, are also contained in

these elements: fire produces a choleric temperament; earth, a
melancholy temperament; air, a sanguine temperament; and
water, a phlegmatic temperament. Over the centuries, the four
elements and their qualities and associations became rich and
powerful symbols for Western magical traditions.

As part of your training in love magic, we recommend
shapeshifting into these elements to experience how earth, air,
fire, and water participate in the universe. In these transforma-
tions, you will learn what powers each element possesses and
what contributions each of the four makes to natural and human life. You will also discover in what ways the elements influence you and your lover, because we all have a personal element based on our sign in the zodiac. The fire signs are Aries,
Leo, and Sagittarius. The earth signs are Taurus, Virgo, and
Capricorn. The air signs are Gemini, Libra, and Aquarius. The
water signs are Cancer, Scorpio, and Pisces.

It's normal to wonder if you and someone else will make a
good match. Sometimes you hear that a fire sign and a water
sign, for example, can't get along because they are naturally
antagonistic. Water destroys fire. But fire can also dry up water,
burn up material objects, and consume air. It would seem that a
fire sign is trouble for everyone! On the other hand, a strong
wind can blow out a fire, and earth can smother fire. So the
other signs aren't helpless. If we explore these antagonisms to
their ultimate conclusions, it may look like everything has the
potential to destroy everything else! A depressing proposition
that might lead us to conclude we should mate only with our
own kind!

The psychological truth here is that any qualities joined
together in a relationship can be volatile. Given the appropriate
circumstances, different personality types might be very incompatible. Any couple can have problems stemming from myriad

sources, of course, but the problems always seem to be influenced to some extent by the person's basic temperament as reflected in the four physical elements.

You can use the elements in love magic to strengthen a relationship and work out problems. Magic operates on both the symbolic and actual planes to effect change in the world. The elements and their symbols are receptacles. Into them we put actual hopes, fears, and problems. The elements become the tools that provide solutions. As facilitators, they operate on the level of consciousness and on the physical level, corresponding to the personality factors that can clash and threaten a relationship. By creating a stronger union between the two elements representing you and your lover, you begin the healing process.

Try the following ten spells to cover every combination of elemental signs, so you will find a spell appropriate for you and your partner. In each spell, the two elements are linked in a ritual manner, providing an opportunity for you to shift consciousness and explore the dynamics of your relationship on another plane, thus gaining insights into what the relationship might need. A by-product of each ritual is a love talisman to use in further magical or sexual rites.

We suggest you always use objects gathered specifically for these rituals and make the gathering of them a ritual in itself. Go on a special quest into the woods or fields to find stone, soil, or sand for earth. Collect water from a spring, river, lake, pond, or waterfall (some rituals suggest drinking the water afterward, so collect your water from a potable source). If you are a city-bound urbanite, buy a special bottle of springwater at a grocery store to use only for this spell. For fire buy a special candle, choosing a color that is your favorite or your lover's (depending on which of you has the fire sign). Air rituals use incense and feathers. Select a scent that you or your lover enjoys. The color of the feathers, and the birds from which they come, can be determined by you or your lover's preferences.

Charge all ritual objects before using them, by neutralizing any unwanted energy that would work against the purpose of the spell and by putting your energy into them. Cast a circle at your altar (or wherever you plan to do the spell), and always go into alpha before shifting consciousness or combining the elements.

Each spell requires a shift of consciousness into one or both of the elements being used. (See Chapter 2 for details.) As you do this be mindful of which element represents you and which your partner. As a working rule, first shift into your element, then, if the spell asks for it, your lover's. A practice I find helpful for shifting consciousness: Recall and say to yourself, once or several times: "I have been alive forever. There is nothing in which I have not been."

Earth and Water

You will need a handful of small pebbles, water, and an attractive bowl or jar. Charge the objects. Place the pebbles in the bowl.

Put your consciousness into your element, and remain there for a while, experiencing what you think and feel like as that element. Then slowly pour the water over the pebbles. As you do, shift your consciousness to experience the other element, and slowly move to the edge of consciousness where the two elements meet. Linger in that altered state of consciousness for a while, experiencing the edge of water and stone. Feel the flow of water over stone from the points of view of both the water and the stone. Then slowly return to ordinary consciousness.

You may want to leave the pebbles in the bowl of water on your altar or in the bedroom until the water evaporates. Or place the water and pebbles in a special jar with a lid. The pebbles can be carried with you, placed under the middle of the mattress where you both sleep, or hidden somewhere in your lover's environment. Or you can divide them up, and give half to your lover in a special bottle or talisman bag. As a couple's ritual, you can drink the water together right before you make love, or put drops of it on your foreheads or other parts of your bodies. You can also sprinkle the water on the bed using a sprig of cedar or evergreen. Or sprinkle it on your lover's clothes.

Earth and Fire

You will need a candle and either a stone or a stick about five to ten inches long. Charge the objects.

Light the candle and watch it burn for a few moments. If you are using a stick, carve what you wish onto it at this point: your names, initials, symbols, runes. Shift consciousness into your element and experience it for a few moments. Take the candle and allow wax to drip onto the stone or stick. Cover the object with as much wax as you feel is appropriate. Experience the edge of consciousness where hot wax and earth-object meet. Feel the interplay of heat and earth from both the wax's point of view (which contains the heat) and that of the stone or stick. Linger there for a while, then return to ordinary consciousness.

Carry the stone or stick as a talisman, bury it, place it under your mattress, or hide it in your lover's environment. Save the candle, and light it the next time you make love. You can also remove the wax and add it to the top of the candle so that it burns again.

Earth and Air

You will need some very small pebbles and incense. Charge them.

Light the incense, and when the smoke is fulsome, hold the pebbles in one hand over it. Slowly and rhythmically transfer the pebbles from hand to hand, so they are smudged on all sides by the incense. Listen to the clicking sound of the pebbles, noting that the element of air carries the sound to your ear. Place your consciousness in the element that represents your sign, and slowly move to the edge of consciousness where air and stone meet. Feel the drift of incense over the stone from both the air's point of view and that of the stone. Experience that state for as long as you wish, then slowly return to ordinary consciousness.

Use the pebbles as talismans. Divide up the pebbles and give half to your lover. Place them under the mattress, or hide them in your lover's environment.

Earth and Earth

Gather a small amount of two different types of soil. Sand can be used for one type, regular soil for the other. Or use pebble-free soil for one and some very small pebbles for the other. Designate one soil to represent you, the other for your lover, based on whatever correspondences you perceive between the soils and the two of you. One soil, for example, may be softer, coarser, weaker, lighter, or darker than the other. Or the correspondences might be based on where you collected the soil: yard, woods, stream bed, hillside, valley, mountaintop, city, country, and so forth. Charge the soils.

Place the two soils in separate bowls at the start of the ritual. When you begin the ritual, place your consciousness into "your" soil and then your partner's. Remain in each for several moments, experiencing each as a separate spot of earth. Then, when the moment feels right, pick up both bowls, and slowly pour the soils together into a third bowl. Let your consciousness experience the blending of the two types of earth and linger there in the "new" soil. Feel the individuality of each soil separately and the new individuality of the two blended together. Then return to ordinary consciousness.

Keep the blend on your altar, or put a small amount into a Baggie to carry with you. You can also scatter part of it on your yard or garden, or put it into a potted plant in the bedroom. Scatter the rest on your lover's yard. When very dry, the soil can be used to gently smudge your foreheads or any other parts of your bodies the next time you make love.

Air and Fire

You will need a candle, incense, and a piece of parchment. Charge the objects. Write both your names or initials on the parchment, or compose a ritual poem, or write a spell that expresses your hopes and dreams for the relationship.

Smudge the parchment over the incense. Shift consciousness to become the air that is scenting and permeating the fibers of the parchment. Move into the edge of consciousness where the fibers and the sweet-scented air become one. Then hold the parchment over the flame, and let it burn. Drop the burning paper into a cauldron or pot, and let your consciousness join the consciousness of the flame as it and the scented air in the paper meet.

Rub the ashes on the bedframe. Smudge your foreheads or other parts of your bodies the next time you make love. Or scatter the ashes in the garden or put them into a potted plant in the bedroom.

Air and Air

You will need two different kinds of incense and two feathers. Let one incense and feather represent you, the others will represent your partner.

Burn both kinds of incense separately, about twelve to fifteen inches apart, and place your consciousness in the air between the two burners. Take a feather in each hand, and slowly waft the incense toward the middle, where your consciousness is, so that the two streams of smoke mingle and become one. Shift consciousness to that mingled stream of sweet-scented air now entering your nose and traveling into your lungs. Stay with it as the oxygen enters the blood and is carried to all parts of your body. Focus especially on the oxygen reaching your genitals, where its energy will be stored to enhance your next love-making session.

The feathers, too, contain the mixture of air. Wear them in your hair. Give one to your partner. Sew the quills together with thread and needle, and hang them over your bed. Place one under each side of the mattress. Use them for brushing your lover's body the next time you make love. Or for tickling!

Air and Water

You will need incense, a feather, and a bowl or chalice of water.

Light the incense, and when it is burning well, smudge the feather, moving it back and forth several times through the stream of smoke. Place your consciousness into your element, and when you have experienced it for a few moments, waft the incense into the water with the feather and gently stir the water with the tip of the feather. Move into the edge of consciousness where the incense-laden air and water merge, possibly on the feather itself. Tarry there in that state of merging consciousness as long as you wish. Feel what it means to be a feather containing a blend of air and water. Then return to an ordinary state.

Drink the water, or share it with your lover the next time you make love. Or pour some of it into the garden or a potted plant in the bedroom. Or keep the water in a jar on your altar. Or sprinkle it over the bed with a sprig of cedar or evergreen. Carry or wear the feather as a talisman, or put it under the mattress in the middle of the bed.

Fire and Water

You will need a candle and a bowl of water. Charge both.

Light the candle and let it burn for a few moments while you shift consciousness into your element. When you are ready, drip wax into the water. Watch the movement of the wax droplets across the surface. Shift to the edge of consciousness where you become the meeting place of hot wax and cool water. Experience the merger of the two elements from the water's point of view and from that of the heat in the wax. Remain there until you decide to return to ordinary consciousness. If you have a question about your relationship, you can scry the pattern of wax droplets on the water when you are finished.

Save the wax droplets and carry them as a talisman, or place them under the mattress. Or melt them in a pot on the stove, and form one clump of wax to use in some ritual way. You can save the wax and the candle for the next time you make love. Burn the candle and add the wax to the top, then let it melt and burn a second time.

Fire and Fire

You will need two candles, one to represent you, the other for your lover.

Light the candles and let them burn for a few moments while you shift consciousness into the flame on your candle. When the time seems right, pick up both candles and hold them so the flames meet and become one flame. (Catch the dripping wax in a bowl.) Experience the addition of your lover's flame as it enters your flame. You will probably lose all sense of where your flame ends and your lover's begins. Let your consciousness incorporate both flames as one, and stay there until you are ready to return to ordinary consciousness.

Save the candles, and light them the next time you make love. You can add the wax to the tops of the candles at that time, or put the wax under the mattress in the middle of the bed. Or hide the wax somewhere in your partner's environment.

Water and Water

You will need three chalices or bowls and water collected from two different sources. If possible, select sources based on correspondences you perceive between them and you and your lover, such as country, city, woods, hillside, valley, lake, stream, waterfall, pond, and so forth. Charge both waters.

Begin the ritual with the water in two separate bowls or chalices. Place your consciousness in the water representing you, and become that water, feeling and thinking as water does. Then shift your consciousness into the water representing your lover. Notice the difference in the experience. When the time seems right, simultaneously pour the water in both bowls into a third bowl. Shift your consciousness to experience the confluence of the two streams of water, and linger in that experience for a while. Then return to ordinary consciousness.

Drink the water yourself, or share it with your lover the next time you make love. Anoint your foreheads, or other parts of your bodies. Sprinkle the water over the bed with a sprig of cedar or evergreen. Sprinkle your lover's clothes with the water. Pour the water out in your garden or into a potted plant in the bedroom, or at your lover's home. Or add it to your bathwater the next time you and your lover take a bath together.

Invoking the Gods and Goddesses

EVERYONE loves an enthusiastic lover, and the world would probably be a better place if we had more of them. The word *enthusiastic* comes from the Greek phrase *en theos,* meaning "in the God" or "the God within." A person *en theos* lives with the power and energy of a God, and might even be thought to be possessed by that God. These God-filled people demonstrate an élan and a zest for life lacking in many ordinary mortals.

Witches have kept alive the practice of invoking the Gods and Goddesses in their rites. To invoke, to "call within," is to summon forth a particular deity, bringing that God's energy into your consciousness where it influences your mind, body, behavior, and ultimately your entire life. Divine energy is always transformative, and with the Gods and Goddesses active within us, we, too, are transformed into better lovers, more sympathetic mates, stronger individuals, more creative partners.

We live in a universe where the powers of the Gods and Goddesses are interlaced through all time and space, all cultures, all individuals. In the mythological worlds each deity has a particular realm—love, war, sovereignty, death, the Otherworld, the sky—but each deity's influence weaves through time and space, connecting with parallel realms in our own lives. In every age the Gods and Goddesses become incarnate in the lives of men and women with whom these divine helpers have a special relationship.

The ancient Gods and Goddesses often intervene in our lives, whether we acknowledge them or not. Without conscious acknowledgment, however, we tend to be oblivious of their intervention. Some people describe this lack of awareness as the death of the old Gods and Goddesses. We say, rather, that the Old Ones are not dead, they are just not incarnate in certain modern men and women. But we live in a universe where change is cyclic, and so it is always possible to bring a particular God or special type of Goddess "back to life" within our deeper selves. Once reincarnated within, that God or Goddess begins to incarnate in our outer lives as well.

When invoked with respect and confidence, the Gods and Goddesses come, eager to share their special power and knowledge. By meditating on them, bringing them into our consciousness at odd moments of the day, we share their unique vision and role in the universe. At such moments we become empowered with their strength. If you are a Witch, you know this. If you are not, this may seem like a strange idea to you. Many modern people have discarded the notion that the Old Ones still exist and that they bring their magic into our lives. If you are skeptical, we suggest you "play along," suspend your disbelief and imagine nature still interwoven with spirit, as described in the many ancient tales and legends from around the world and from your own ancestors who lived close to nature and understood the secret spirits of the earth and sky.

It is important to recognize the God-energy activating us on different occasions because, as Carl Jung and his students have pointed out, even an unacknowledged God or Goddess (he called them "archetypes") will demand its due, operating as a predisposition governing positive and negative patterns of behavior and emotion. Clearly, the unrecognized Gods and Goddesses within us can, if we are unaware of them, destroy our relationships. On the other hand, they can, as they so often do in ancient tales, rescue us.

Jungian therapist Jean Shimodo Bolen has written that "knowledge of the gods is a source of personal empowerment" because some Gods need to be liberated within us, others need to be restrained. When we try to cut off and bury them, she warns, we bury them alive. Bolen's two volumes *Goddesses in Everywoman* and *Gods in Everyman* are important works, which we recommend to readers wishing to explore these ideas more thoroughly. We are indebted to Bolen's insights for some of the concepts in this chapter.

Everyone serious about using magic to enhance and strengthen their relationships will do well to confront the Gods and Goddesses influencing their lives, liberating beneficial energies and restraining the potentially harmful. As Bolen points out, some Gods and Goddesses are active in your life on certain occasions, others cast their spells at other times. Different stages of life and different stages of a man or woman's relationship stir up different Gods and Goddesses. Bolen also points out that we can activate some aspects or powers of a God or Goddess without activating others. These are wise principles to keep in mind when invoking the Gods and Goddesses for love.

For example, if you read through the Goddess sections and realize your personality and approach to life is akin to the Hearth Goddesses—wives, mothers, homemakers—and your husband seems to be similar to a Trickster God—footloose, adventurous, restless, unreliable—you can see the potential conflict in your relationship. You have several options. One, activate within yourself a Goddess more sympathetic to your husband, say a Goddess of the Hunt, or activate the more playful aspects of a Love Goddess. Two, call upon your Hearth Goddess protector to teach you ways to accommodate your "homey qualities" to a man who is eager to wander the open road.

We have grouped the Gods and Goddesses into categories based on specific powers and energies. In doing this we keep alive the most ancient Celtic tradition of worshiping patterns of divine energy first and their human representations second. Before there was a Goddess of the Hearth, there was fire; before Mars, there was war; before Venus, there was love; before Loki, there was luck; and so forth. It is believed that all ancient cultures worshiped in this primal way and only later created physical, human representations of these divine energy patterns. The Celts began sculpting and carving physical representations of their Gods and Goddesses only in Roman times, inspired possibly by Roman artists creating images of Celtic deities to complement their own pantheon of Gods and Goddesses.

It has been said that all the Gods and Goddesses are one God/dess and that all mythologies flower from the same mythic soil: the hunt, the quest for fire, birth and death, the seedtime and harvest, the rites of passage, and so forth. In all cultures, we find the same great mythic themes in one form or another, just as we find the same Gods and Goddesses wearing different masks. Their faces may change; but their powers are eternal.

In whatever cultural form you honor the Gods and God-desses, you will find those forms in our rituals. If you prefer, as did the Celts, to honor them as archetypal patterns, such as the Lord of Wind, the Lady of the Wild Things, the Spirit of the Well, the God of Ecstasy, you will be able to do the rituals free from any particular cultural designation.

The best way to approach this chapter is to read through the descriptions of all the categories of Gods if you are a man, all the Goddesses if you are a woman. Each group of deities is discussed in terms of (1) realms of power, (2) the personality and temperament of the lovers influenced by the deities in each category, and (3) a ritual for invoking the power of the Gods or Goddesses in that category followed by the natural objects that can be used in spells, rituals, and your daily life.

Following Bolen's advice, feel free to call upon a God or Goddess for powers other than the ones we have chosen to discuss. The Gods and Goddesses are far richer and more com-plex than our thumbnail sketches of them, and you can use your own knowledge of them to create rituals suited to your purposes. Also, you may discover (as do most people) that you recognize aspects of yourself in more than one deity. This is normal since, as Taliesin has said, we have been alive forever; there is nothing in which we have not been. Work with more than one deity to strengthen and empower different aspects of yourself.

Jean Bolen writes: "There are gods and goddesses in every person. Through them, you glean that moment of insight when something you intuitively know about yourself connects with a clear image and articulate words. Like looking into a mirror and seeing our own features for the first time, this flash can reveal what others react to in you, and show you to yourself more clearly" (*Gods in Everyman,* p. xi).

Enjoy meeting the Gods and Goddesses. They are models of your higher self. They know their connections with the cosmos and the harmony of all created things. They understand their perfections and their limitations, their strengths and their weaknesses. In rituals, you can meet these deities by working and playing with the physical elements representing their realms of power and knowledge. They may show you things about yourself you never dreamed existed or things you have always known, but have lost awhile.

THE GODS

Sky Gods

REALMS

Sky Gods are the Lords of the Sky. Their domain includes wind, thunder, lightning, rain, hail, storms, and weather patterns. Often the Sky God is the chief God of a pantheon since the sky is all-encompassing, ever present, and contains primary resources necessary for all life, namely, sunlight and rain. Some Sky Gods, such as Zeus, Jehovah, and Jupiter, make their dwelling high in the mountains or on a particular mountaintop close to the sky and the forces of weather, favorable vantage points for observing earthly life below. Associated with these deities are the lightning bolt, stars, planets, galaxies, meteors, oak trees struck by lightning and their leaves, the hammer, and the eagle.

Some of the more prominent Sky Gods are Zeus, Jehovah, Jupiter, Thor, Odin, Horus, Nwyvre, Taranis, and Nuada.

LOVERS

Men ruled by Sky Gods tend to be strong-willed males, enamored with their sense of control and power. They get what they want and can be violent and abusive when thwarted. Like the Sky Gods, they take decisive action; they seldom mope around or brood over their decisions. Rarely do they have second thoughts or doubts after acting. In general, if you are this type, you value your ability to reason and can be expected to act in reasonable ways, according to your standards. You tend to be critical of others and often sit in judgment.

As a rule, Sky God lovers are not very intimate. Aloof and aloft, you tend to be distant observers of life, quick to judge the affairs of other men and women. Emotionally distant, you react from the head rather than the heart. You are probably not very connected to the earthiness of human life. Although you get riled up in specific emotional encounters, you are usually not very passionate or personal in relationships. You can, however, be extremely seductive and aggressive in lovemaking. Thinking of yourself as "quasi supreme," you do not want to be bound by the same standards of morality as others. Lovers ruled by Sky Gods can be extremely unfaithful partners. Zeus, for example, was a notorious philanderer. A fierce heterosexual lover and the father of many children by Goddesses and mortal women, he also enjoyed a homoerotic fling with Ganymede, a beautiful young boy with whom he fell in love and carried off to Olympus to be the cupbearer to the Gods.

RITUAL

Sky Gods can be invoked to bring more control and authority into your relationships when you feel used, dominated, or manipulated. Care should be taken, however, to activate only sufficient power to correct the imbalance, not so much that you become the domineering partner.

A ritual to invoke a Sky God should be performed outdoors if possible, on top of a high hill or mountain or near a cliff. A windy day is perfect.

Take a ritual sword, knife, wand, or staff. If you make a staff or wand especially for this ritual, use oak (sacred to Thor) and inscribe lightning bolts on it. Men who invoke Thor specifically may wish to use a ritual hammer.

Stand on the hilltop and spread your arms to the sky, holding your ritual tool in the right hand. Let the wind blow against your face, and breathe deeply and rhythmically. Become aware of your breathing, and place your consciousness on the fresh wind filling your lungs and body. This wind is the power of the God.

At some point, when it feels right, grasp your tool in both hands and hold it in front of you, pointed upward at a forty-five-degree angle, extended over the view or scene below. Place your consciousness on the tip of the tool, and become aware that it is attracting the power of the God, like a lightning rod attracts electrical bolts. In this way, you are charging the tool to take back with you and be a future source of the God's energy.

Invocation: "Gods of the Sky (or specific name), I invoke your power to (state your intention) and draw your energy into me and my wand. You are the wind that blows around my body, and you are the air that strengthens my blood and bones. I accept your strength and your power and make it mine."

When invoking the Sky Gods in ritual or in daily life, use the following tools: *herbs*—cinnamon, allspice, cotton, cloves, fennel, dill, myrtle, savory, shepherd's rod; *stones*—turquoise, lapis lazuli, amethyst, rutilated quartz, fire opal, modavite, and meteorite; *oils*—jasmine, honeysuckle, patchouli, vetivert, birch, geranium, pear, mistletoe; *colors*—red, yellow, blue, royal blue, purple, gold; *metals*—platinum, silver.

Sun Gods

REALMS

Sun Gods rule with the light and energy of the sun. Like the Sky Gods, their realm is the celestial firmament. Their primary source of power is fire. Since they share the kingdom of the sky with moon deities, their time of influence is limited to the daylight hours. They are, however, most approachable at dawn, dusk, or high noon. Associated with them are chariots (sometimes fiery) drawn by horses or swans, the hawk, the phoenix, archery, music, poetry, the arts, gold crowns and rings. Prominent Sun Gods include Apollo, Lugh, Balder, Helios, Marduk, Mithra, Ra, and Vishnu.

LOVERS

Men ruled by Sun Gods are bright, sunny, shining personalities, but they can be arrogant and distant. They are often fair-haired, privileged sons of powerful fathers. Sun God males favor logical thinking over feelings or knowledge from the heart. They are extremely goal-oriented (headed west each day!), and strive for moderation and balance in their lives rather than excess.

If you are influenced by a Sun God, you probably look for purity and clarity in relationships. You may also seek the same type of personality in a mate: a radiant, bright, clear-thinking, goal-oriented woman or man. In this way, your love of balance extends even into relationships. Since you fall in love "from the head," as it were, you like your partners to be head-people rather than heart-people. In fact, a certain amount of narcissism may characterize the relationship based on things you have in common. You will share similar interests and mirror each other in various ways. As a Sun God lover, you may not exhibit much emotion or be very erotic. But you probably have a strong need to sire noble and beautiful children. If you are gay, you might take warning from Apollo's tragic romance with the Spartan athlete Hyacinth, whom he accidentally killed when the God's discus hit the young man in the head. Play safe!

RITUAL

Call upon Sun Gods either to initiate something new in your life or relationships, or to banish and end problems. The Gods' forte lies in knowing what is appropriate for your goals and for bringing balance and harmony into your life. Dawn is the auspicious time for rituals to begin something new; dusk is best for banishing. Perform the ritual at high noon to address the sun at its most potent moment. Choose some spot outdoors or at a window where you can see the dawn or the sunset.

Light a white or bright yellow candle, preferably a thick, short candle, rather than a tall, slender taper. Spend a few moments allowing the light of the new day or the rays from the setting sun to penetrate the candle flame, and put your awareness into the flame. Slowly, shift your consciousness to the shape of the flame, and spend a few moments letting this flame-consciousness spread throughout your body and into your aura, until it, too, is the shape of flame or fire. Identify with fire, until you are able to think and feel as fire does.

When you have become fire, allow the energy of the Sun God to warm your body and mind. Experience it strengthening you for the specific intention of your ritual.

For a dawn ritual, begin about ten to fifteen minutes before sunrise, and at the first glimpse of the sun over the horizon, switch your gaze from the candle flame to the sun's rays, and invoke the God until the sun is completely visible. Invocation: "Hail, to the God of the Dawn (or specific name). I sit in readiness for a new day. I seek the power or skill to (name your goal or intention). Fire of the Sun, Light of the Sun, Burning Energy of the Sun, fill me with your strength. Empower me to (name your goal). Enlighten me with understanding and clarity in my relationships and all my endeavors."

For a sunset ritual, become the fire, then switch your gaze to the setting sun, almost on the horizon, and watch it drop beneath the earth's rim. Then shift your gaze back to the candle, and make the invocation: "Farewell, God of the Day (or specific name). I send out into your burning heat (name what you wish to banish). Fire of the Sun, Light of the Sun, take these troubles away and transform their power to harm me (or name your lover) into neutral energy that will return to the universe." As you say this, send all negative thoughts and feelings to the horizon where the red, fiery glow consumes all harmful energies.

For a noon ritual, a candle is not needed. In fact, if you are outside, you will not even see its flame in the bright sunlight. Stand and face the sun in the zenith or (on a cloudy day) the section of the sky where the sun is at noon. (This varies depending on the time of year.) Close your eyes and turn your face toward the sun. Spread your legs, and raise your arms upward at each side to shoulder level, palms up. This is the Pentacle Stance, a posture to instill confidence and power. Invoke a Sun God, such as the Celtic God Lugh, the "many skilled God." Say, "This is the time of noon, the midpoint of the day's work. Strengthen me, God of the Sun, God of Skill and Strength. Help me to ride swiftly through the rest of this day, and return at evening with energy and enthusiasm for the things of night."

With your eyes still closed, envision a ball of golden fire leave the sun and speed downward to hover over your head. From the fireball, two streams of light and energy strike the palms of your hands. Feel them tingle, and allow the light to course up your arms, across your shoulders, and into your head and your heart, filling your entire body with strength and energy.

At the end of each ritual, allow your attention to shift back to the spot where you are sitting or standing, and reenter your ordinary consciousness.

When invoking the Sun Gods in ritual or in daily life, use the following tools: *colors*—yellow and gold; *stones*—citrine, cat's-eye, amber, aventurine, red-orange agate, red jasper; *herbs*—sunflower, celandine, ash, frankincense, marigold, bay, rosemary; *oils*—heliotrope, almond, chamomile, olive, sapphron; *metals*—gold, brass.

Sea Gods

REALMS

The spiritual home of the Gods of the Sea are large bodies of water. But we include in this tribe of Gods those with domains in swift rivers, deep lakes, powerful waterfalls, and fast-moving streams. Sea Gods rule storms at sea, and are associated with earthquakes, tidal waves, and floods. They are what some cultures call "Earthshaker." In their realms we find bulls, horses, dolphins, whales, ships, seashells, and tridents. Sea Gods include Poseidon, Neptune, Aegir, Dylan, Manannan mac Lyr, Njord.

LOVERS

Males influenced by Sea Gods can have turbulent personalities, often hiding beneath a placid surface. They are men of intense emotion and temperament, often bad-tempered, ever ready to erupt. As water can be destructive, so can their energy when stirred to anger. They can harbor grudges and seek revenge with great fury. And yet their oceanic natures can bring a depth of feeling and instinct to relationships often lacking in celestial personalities. If you are Sea God–oriented, you may be in your glory when stirring up a tempest, but you are also the power that calms a storm. In spite of your ability to roar and rage, you are also the deep womb of the sea, a place of nurturance and healing. A Sea God male has a hidden, "maternal" side.

As a lover you may dominate your partner with your emotional intensity. Your strong sexual appetites can be frightening to others who do not share them or who forget how quickly your emotions can change. Your relationships may be stormy. You may have a tendency, like Sea Gods, to wreak your vengeance on lovers who cross you. Influenced by a water deity, you mate well with strong, earthy women. As a gay lover, you may, like Poseidon, fall in love with a younger man whom you would like to carry off to your Mount Olympus.

RITUAL

Men ruled by the Sea God Poseidon will most likely want to draw on his power to calm storms and divert tempests. Recognizing the more negative aspects of the Sea God within yourself and allying yourself with the God in order to understand those stormy emotional depths will provide insight into your relationships and teach ways to prevent or sublimate your turbulent side. A solution: Many hurricanes blow themselves out before reaching land.

Witches are able to call up waves, increase their size, and divert them from ships and harbors. This ritual draws on those skills (innate in all of us) and teaches you how to develop them further. If you put your consciousness into the waves or tempest, especially that part of your consciousness harboring your turbulent side, you can send it out to sea where it will not harm you or your lover. Or if you seek to stir up greater emotion in a lover, transform the energy you derive from the waves and tempests into an appropriate, benevolent form and project it toward her or him.

A Sea God ritual should be done by the seashore, a large lake, or a swift, deep river. A deep bath filled with sea salt will substitute if you do not live near a body of water. Place a large seashell next to each ear and listen to the ocean roar for several minutes. As you do so, close your eyes, count yourself into alpha. See the waves pounding on a rocky shore, watch a storm form out over the sea, experience the wind and fury of a hurricane. (At some point you may want to put the seashells down, and lie down on the shore or bank, but continue to keep your consciousness focused on the power of the sea.) Allow the emotions of anger or vengeance to rise up in you, letting them become the wind and waves. Let them blow themselves to their maximum intensity. When it feels right, invoke the Sea God: "Gods of the Sea (or specific name), blow these destructive forces in me far out from shore. Calm my turbulent depths. Give me the strength to remain placid and tranquil in my relationship with (name lover). Teach me how to draw only on your positive qualities, and mine the deep instinctual powers of my soul to provide strength for (lover's name)."

After an invocation along these lines, direct the tempest you have been holding in your consciousness to dissipate. Be aware of the help you receive from the Sea God. The wind will subside, the waves retreat, the clouds thin, and the sun will come out to shine brilliantly on the surface of the water. Become that blend of sunlight and water, and remain in it for a few moments. Then return to ordinary consciousness.

When invoking the Sea Gods in ritual or in daily life, use the following tools: *stones*—pearl, mother-of-pearl, aquamarine, shells, coral, smooth or tumbled pebbles from a stream; *oils*—pear, peach, betony, lily, lotus, camphor; *colors*—light green and blue, sand colors, lavender, sea green; *herbs*—lily, water lily, seaweed, watercress, kelp, sea salt, moonwort, lotus; *metals*—silver.

Gods of the Underworld

Realms

Gods of the Underworld rule regions of the earth that are hidden, dark, deep, mysterious, and (under ordinary circumstances) inaccessible. As Gods of the Dead, they share their abode with the souls passed into the Otherworld. Although they may seem terrifying deities, sulking in murky depths, they are also the Guardians of fabulous treasures. Pluto's world is the world of buried treasure; it is also the place of the deep unconscious containing many truths and secrets of existence. Underworld Gods are guides and protectors for journeyers into and out of those hidden realms, where ancient wisdom and knowledge of the earth and the meaning of mortality may be attained by those brave enough to enter there. Gods of the Underworld include Hades, Pluto, the Dagda, Odin, Anubis, Arawn, and Samhain.

Lovers

Men influenced by the Gods of the Netherworld tend to be reclusive, introverted, content to lead a deep interior life. But as in the story of Hades and Persephone, whoever comes under their influence (in mythic terms, eats the pomegranate) is bonded to them and eventually acquires knowledge and power of the Underworld realms. In other words, their partners can learn from them and come to share their interior lives. In general, Underworld men have little need for society and keep their social involvement to a minimum. They are often unexpressive and lacking in self-esteem. In social situations they hold back, seem to be invisible, lack a forthcoming persona to which others can easily relate. On the positive side, these men enjoy solitude and are at home in the vast regions of the unconscious where they find their source of creativity, insight, and cosmic truth. Here is the darkness where the seed will grow.

If you are influenced by Gods of the Underworld, you may have little experience as a lover. But when you fall in love, you come on strong and tend to rush into relationships. You are probably not into dating and flirting and playing the game of romance. You see what you want and you go for it. On the other hand, periods of celibacy come easy to you, and a deep interior life almost demands that you not dissipate too much energy in sexual and romantic escapades. Your depth of personality can make you a wonderful soulmate.

RITUAL

Gods of the Underworld can be invoked to acquire appreciation of any natural reticence or shyness in romantic relationships, or to overcome these traits. They can also be called upon during times of celibacy or loneliness to inspire the best use of your interior powers.

Rituals should be performed either in a cave or under a rock shelf, by a hollow tree, or near any large, deep opening into the earth. Begin a steady beat on a small drum. Sit on the ground, resting against a wall or tree so you can drum and be relaxed at the same time. (If you have someone to drum for you, all the better.) Go into alpha and let your consciousness sink into the beat of the drum until it energizes you, and takes you lower and lower into yourself. Then visualize your spirit body descending through the cave or opening into the earth, and quickly you will be in a tunnel leading deep into the earth. Proceed down it.

You will emerge in an underground chamber filled with the

kinds of objects you would select to furnish a secret study, workshop, den, or office. Here is where you can do magic. Here is where you can indulge the reclusive side of your personality. Spend some time inspecting, handling, or playing with one or more of the objects you find in this chamber. Notice how at ease you feel, secure and content to be alone for a while. Indulge these feelings and draw their energy deeply into you. Then call upon the Gods.

Invocation: "Gods of the Underworld (or specific name), Powers of the Deepest Earth, Keepers of the Deep Secrets of Life, grant the wisdom to empower my life with the knowledge I learn when alone. Give me confidence to share my deepest sense of self with others (or name partner). Make me confident that the hidden treasures of my life are valuable to others. I invoke your power to grow and thrive in secret places and the courage to emerge and bring your blessings to others."

When you have spent enough time in this chamber in the Lower World, return up the tunnel and emerge at the spot where you began. Continue drumming for a few moments, slowing down the beat. At some point, end the journey with a few powerful drumbeats.

When invoking the Gods of the Underworld in ritual or in daily life, use the following tools: *herbs*—elm, hemp, juniper, Solomon's seal, mushrooms, mandrake, oak, apple, any root from a deep-rooted tree such as willow, ash, pine; *metals*—steel, silver, gold, pewter, copper, iron; *stones*—jasper, coal, stalagmite, salt, kunnite, lava, shale, slate, volcanic stone, marble, hematite, quartz, brown agate, fossils; *oils*—comfrey, musk, lemon, wisteria, storax, cedar, myrrh, frankincense; *colors*—brown, black, emerald green, gray, charcoal, beige, sand.

Gods of War

REALMS

War Gods rule battlefields, athletic events, and (we have a sneaking suspicion) Wall Street. Their domains are those areas of human activity requiring aggression, physical power and strength, assertiveness. They champion heroes and warriors. True, most Gods can and do fight, but specific Gods of War embody the spirit of the fight, the battle ethic, the commitment to struggle for goals achieved only by physical force. Their talismans are spear, sword, shield, and drum. Gods of War include Mars, Ares, Assur, Indra, Odin, Tyr, Mithra, Tiwaz, Hesus.

LOVERS

As expected, fiery tempers make men ruled by War Gods volatile and assertive. They are quick to explode when attacked, but just as quick to avenge and protect others. They favor physical strengths and skills, and promote teamwork, cooperation, and the spirit of comradeship. Often type A personalities, they shine under pressure. Impulsiveness can lead them into action without thinking. At their worst, War God lovers can be childish brawlers or vengeful thugs.

If a God of War dwells prominently in your psyche, you may tend to lock horns with your lover in frequent spats and fights. Of course, as the old saying goes, half the fun of fighting is making up, and War God males are terrific lovers when calmed down after a fight and beginning the healing process. You tend to be an earthy, physical lover, but not very spiritual or mystical. Relationships are characterized by a lot of physical activity, possibly sports, athletics, games, and other competitive pursuits. You may be into S & M relationships, and need to control the dark side that can border on physical abuse.

Ritual

Rituals to honor the Gods of War within you might simply call upon them to ignite your more assertive, aggressive, or competitive spirit for some specific purpose; for example, when you are in competition with another man, or when you just need to be more assertive in a relationship. More frequently, however, War God rituals are necessary to release aggressive feelings and hot tempers before they become uncontrollable battle frenzy, disrupting or destroying a relationship.

This ritual requires a drum or an old sword and shield. If you don't have an old sword and shield lying around, you might convert a trash can lid and a wooden broom handle, the way you did as a boy playing Knights of the Round Table. Do not think these items are a childish substitute! The petulant, hot-tempered child in us, often the source of our battle frenzy, can cause our partners grief. Using a trash can lid and old broom handle will conjure up and release that childishness, maybe better than a genuine sword and shield would.

In an open field or yard, begin to beat the sword on the shield (or beat the drum), and count yourself into alpha. Begin dancing to the beat. Start slowly if you feel self-conscious, swaying to the beat, gradually moving your feet up and down as if marching. In time, you will loosen up and dance with gusto. Let yourself go. The more you can physically release anger, vengeance, abusiveness, or violent impulses by means of dance, the better. If you are dancing to increase a healthy assertiveness, focus on the energy building up within yourself. If you feel silly dancing by yourself, recall this old Celtic proverb: "Never give a sword to a man who can't dance."

When you have finished, lie down on the ground and invoke the Gods of War: "Gods of Battle and Strife, I lie here subdued, but not defeated. I have driven out my anger, but not my passion. I am no longer a threat to others, but I am not powerless. I honor and nurture the strength and fire of the spiritual warrior. I resolve, with your help, to return to my life, a gentler, calmer warrior, committed to fighting only the good fight."

Stay on the ground until your breath returns and you are completely rested. Then you can rise with perfect grace and confidence.

When invoking the Gods of War in ritual or in daily life, use the following tools: *stones*—azurite, geode, golden beryl, red jasper, fire opal, garnet, hematite, iron, ruby, gold jewelry; *herbs* —aloes, dragon's blood, mastic, tarragon, thistle, benzoin, curry, broom, cayenne pepper, chili powder, nettle, peppercorns; *oils*—honeysuckle, storax, myrrh, hyssop, coriander, pine, orchid; *colors*—red, black, burgundy, white; *metals*—iron, gold, brass.

Gods of Ecstasy

REALMS

In this tribe of Gods we include both Gods of Madness and Drunkenness, such as Dionysius and Silenus; Saturn, whose festival of orgies includes sexual role reversals; Gods of the Dance, such as Krishna; and the many Nature and Fertility Gods including Cernunnos, Frey, Osiris, Pan, and Attis. These

Gods contain a strong fountain of instinctual knowledge and wisdom that gushes forth to nourish both human society and the cultivated land. They are the Gods of seedtime and harvest, whose crops are poetry, music, drama, dance, and the arts, as well as the crops of the field. They are Gods of Ecstasy because their power works spontaneously, erratically, instinctually, unencumbered by rational thought.

LOVERS

Men ruled by Gods of Ecstasy display a wonderful paradox. They can appear wild, mad, enthusiastic, drunk on wine or some personal passion, and yet this divine chaos can bring forth great blessings for others when it doesn't get out of hand. Extremely creative, they have a sense of specialness, a sense of boyish intensity, an ability to go into trance and altered states of consciousness. They are mystical wanderers through their own personal visions of reality. Obviously they are not governed by standard rules and social mores, and for this reason their influence must be limited, as in ancient Greece and Rome to certain times of the year. They embody intense opposites, loving life yet recklessly flirting with death and the unconscious. But from these polarities come great insight, wisdom, and creativity.

Gods of Ecstasy are fun! When they appear in your psyche, you become sensual, erotic, spontaneous, free-spirited, ready to try anything at least once. You enjoy game-playing and make-believe and the chance to act out sexual fantasies. But you can also be promiscuous, unfaithful, restless, always hungry for new experiences (often with someone other than your primary partner). You have the power to provide ecstatic sexual experiences for your partners, but you can easily grow morose and bored when ecstasy fades.

RITUAL

It almost seems like a contradiction to give instructions for a ritual to honor the Gods of Ecstasy and Spontaneity, so I'm going merely to suggest a setting and let you decide what you will do there.

The setting: a cultivated field, meadow, or wild and inaccessible place, preferably on a warm night under a full moon. Ideally, secluded enough to do the ritual unclothed or with a minimum of clothing (loincloth and sandals, or their equivalent). Accessories: a jug of wine or grape juice, goat cheese, a bunch of grapes, and coarse, multigrained bread or rolls. Drums, rattles, Pan pipes, flutes, and tambourines are required (or a cassette player and tapes of wild, pagan, orgiastic music). Make headbands out of leaves, vines, or wildflowers. Paint erotic fertility symbols on your chest, face, arms, legs, and back. Cut staffs about your own height, and tie leaves and flowers to the tops of them.

Suggested activities: Drink the wine, eat the goat cheese, stomp on a few grapes and eat the rest, break and share the bread with your partners, dance barefoot, chant, howl at the moon, become aware of the erotic nature of the earth and the night, your own erotic qualities, and perhaps those of your companion.

When invoking the Gods of Ecstasy in ritual or in daily life, use the following tools: *stones*—sugilite, black tourmaline, amethyst, rose quartz, clear quartz; *herbs*—peach, catnip, blackberry, sycamore, thyme, pennyroyal, dittany of Crete, lotus, Solomon's seal, Saint-John's-wort, mandrake, grape leaf; *oils*—violet, strawberry, cherry, storax, lotus, sandalwood, patchouli, rose; *colors*—red, black, purple; *metals*—platinum, silver, gold.

Trickster Gods

REALMS

Every culture has some type of Trickster figure. Hermes, Mercury, and Loki are European Trickster Gods. In North America, native peoples found these Trickster deities in certain animals: Raven, Coyote, Hare. In Hindu societies, Krishna was the independent, mischievous, impudent God, the most human and charming of the Gods. The magicians Merlin, Thoth, and Taliesin also fall into this grouping. Because of their repeated success in getting out of scrapes, Tricksters are the Gods of Good Luck. The classic Trickster Gods are typically messengers, and their haunts are roads, highways, waysides, and crossroads. Today they are still honored as patrons of travelers. Stone markers or cairns erected at crossroads are their shrines. One of their important responsibilities: to meet and lead the souls of the departed into the Afterlife.

LOVERS

Tricksters are deceiving, playful, cunning, impulsive. Men ruled by them are great escape artists, often falling into tragic–comic situations where there seems to be no way out. But they find one. Extremely inventive, Tricksters' minds dart from idea to idea, like quicksilver, another name for the element mercury, named after the Roman God.

A Trickster male tends to be a bachelor, lacking commitment to any one mate for any length of time. He seldom settles down and marries. Under the influence of a Trickster God, you can disappear for long periods of time, seeking novelty and adventure on your own. If you pair up with a partner ruled by a

Trickster (assuming he will tolerate your companionship!), you are in for surprises. Be ready for a variety of unpredictable escapades. Trickster lovers can be very seductive and charming, but prone to lies and deception. They are good at manipulation. They are also not beyond thievery and fraud.

RITUAL

One of the positive influences of Trickster Gods is to upset rigid, ossified life-patterns. Call on them when you need to break out of unproductive or simply boring ruts.

Hermes is often depicted wearing a broad-brimmed hat and shoes with wings. We suggest that for this ritual you wear an old broad-brimmed hat, carry a walking stick, and etch or paint wings on your shoes (on the soles or in an inconspicuous spot on the back of the heels, if you are worried about others seeing them). Choose a crossroads out in the country, and either walk to it or drive, but leave your car about a mile down the road.

Your objective is to build a small cairn or pile of stones at the crossroads, so if you select a place without stones or rocks nearby, collect them from somewhere else and bring them with you, preferably in a backpack. Or gather them as you walk to the crossroads. The stones need not be large and heavy, or even very many. Size is not important.

As you approach the crossroads, meditate on the God of Travelers, the Guide of Souls, the Merry Prankster of the deities. Use the time to examine your life and determine where you could be looser, more fun-loving, more impulsive. When you arrive at your destination, bless each stone, and pile them up in a small heap to honor the God.

Invocation: "Gods of the Crossroads (or specific name), I build this cairn to witness to my presence here at your crossroads. Teach me to be alert to choices, to options, to different and more exciting directions for my life or my relationship with (name your partner). Let me be a source of fun and merriment for (name). Bring into our relationship your spirit of curiosity, adventure, and unpredictability."

Bless the site, and as you return, run and skip (that's right, you heard correctly, *skip*) at least part of the way back to your car or home.

When invoking the Trickster Gods in ritual or in daily life, use the following tools: *stones*—holy stones, sun stones, chrysocolla, pyrite, watermelon or black tourmaline, emerald, a stone from Tintagle or Merlin's cave in England, any stone found on a pathway, diamond, moonstone, rutilated quartz; *colors*—pied/dappled/multicolors, crazy designs, patches of black and white; *herbs*—clover, dittany of Crete, jasmine, mustard seed, mistletoe, fennel, dill, caraway, pomegranate, mushroom, trefoil, horehound; *oils*—sandalwood, benzoin, storax, lavender, lily of the valley, narcissus, wisteria, lobelia, apricot; *metals*—gold, silver.

Gods of Crafts

REALMS

Inventors, artisans, sculptors, and builders, the Gods of the Crafts rule forge, anvil, or any workshop where raw materials become beautiful or useful objects. They have a special relationship with fire, since historically it is the power of fire that melts and fuses metals and hardens and glazes sculpted clay. Their domain tends to be underground in the fiery bowels of the earth, in Nature's furnace. Some cultures attribute volcanic activity to their influence. Craft Gods include Hephaestus, Vulcan, Lug, Wayland the Smith, Ptah.

LOVERS

Gods of the Crafts rule men who love to tinker and engage in creative, manual work. For them, work is more than just a way to make a living. They get an important joy out of it, and if they do not earn their living by their special skills, they may spend hours using these skills in an appropriate hobby. Their craft gives their lives meaning. Hephaestus was crippled and rejected by the other Gods, and men influenced by him may be loners, psychologically wounded and lacking self-esteem, using their craft to avoid society and relationships.

If these Gods are active in your psyche, you may need a lot of privacy and time alone. You can often go for long periods without sex, sublimating sexual drives into your craft. Introverted and shy, you require a partner who can lure you out of your preoccupations with work or hobbies, although she or he will have to respect your strong need for solitude and creativity. You may be attracted to partners who are willing to take care of your daily necessities.

RITUAL

The Gods of the Crafts provide a healthy balance to all-consuming and suffocating relationships. Everyone needs his own space at certain times. If you are a man without enough time to yourself, this ritual may begin a new era in your relationship.

For this ritual you will need a pack of modeling clay or Silly Putty or some other claylike material that can be shaped and formed by hand, and a large nail. Go into the cellar or basement near a furnace or fireplace. Light eight candles, placed in the four directions and cross quarters to form a ring around you. Sit in the middle, take a few deep breaths, go into alpha, and hold the clay in your hands, putting your attention into the clay and experiencing what it means to be clay.

Invoke the Gods: "Gods of the Crafts (or specific name), I shape this material from the earth in your name, and I ask for skill to make it a thing of beauty. I form it to be a totem of my creativity and my need to be productive in my hours alone. I press into it my love for and commitment to (name your partner)."

Then mold the clay into a simple figure. It need not be elaborate or representational of any specific thing. Any simple form or figure will do. When you are satisfied with it, etch your name and that of your partner, or your initials, into the sculpture with the nail.

While still in alpha, experience the clay now as the unique shape you have given it. Direct your awareness particularly to the names or initials. Feel them etched into the clay, and appreciate how they are now part of this clay. When it feels right, come back to ordinary consciousness, and put out the candles.

Put the figurine where you will see it, reminding you to carve out enough space in your relationship so you do not become consumed by it. It stands as your commitment to spend more time alone or to devote more time to personal hobbies that give you pleasure and in their own small way give life meaning. Recall that both you and your lover's initials are on the sculpture, remembering that the time spent on your own is not selfish time but time of renewal, so you return to your partner fresh and eager to be together again.

When invoking Gods of Crafts in ritual or in daily life, use the following tools: *stones*—quartz, emerald, sapphire, cobalt, rhodochrosite, clay; *herbs*—ash, cinammon, maple, borage, rose, rose hips, oak; *oils*—lemon, lime, rose, magnolia; *colors*—bronze, copper, pewter; *metals*—gold, silver, iron, brass.

THE GODDESSES

Goddesses of the Hunt

REALMS

A Goddess of the Hunt is the Lady of the Wild Things, the Goddess of the Crescent Moon, the Lady of the Forest. She is a virgin, in the archaic sense of that term, a woman independent and complete in herself. Whether she takes a lover or not is up to her, and should she do so, it in no way violates her maiden status. She is the perennial maiden, aloof, happy, and single in her sylvan haunts. Goddesses of the Hunt are also the patrons of athletes and competitive sport. Goddesses of the Hunt and the Wild Things include Artemis, Diana, Aradia, Skadi, Macha.

LOVERS

Women influenced by Goddesses of the Hunt are independent, free-thinking, free-acting. Eccentric in their lifestyle, they do not derive personal self-worth from what others think about them. They may have a yearning to return to nature or live alone in the countryside. As girls, many are "tomboys" and may become athletes or sportswomen or retain a fondness and interest in sports as adults. Artemis types make good sisters, and enjoy playing that role with other women and close male friends. But they can be very competitive.

Goddesses of the Hunt may influence you to lead a chaste life, although not without occasional love affairs. You may tend to be aloof and not too emotionally intimate, preferring to strike up a brother–sister relationship with a man, even when he becomes your lover. You may play hard to get, often so involved in a career or hobby you have little time for love. Sex for you may be more of a sport or recreation, rather than a form of commitment. Lesbians influenced by the Hunt Goddesses may look upon sex as an important ingredient of friendship with another woman, rather than the foundation for a deeply committed relationship.

Ritual

Call upon the Goddesses of the Hunt for a more independent attitude toward love, for help to become less possessive of a lover, or to overcome the feeling that you must constantly have a lover to make life worth living. These Goddesses can give you the strength to choose either to have a lover or to live without one. Their influence will also give you a freer, more confident attitude toward career and friendships.

Choose a day during the new virgin moon, and go for a leisurely walk in a natural setting, such as a woods or a city park. While walking, keep the Goddess of the Hunt in your mind and heart, feel her presence leading you onward. Hunt for five leaves, three twigs, and one or more bird feathers. Make the search for these a quest, for they will become power objects for courage and confidence to live according to your own lights.

When you return home, set up an altar in an area of some special significance for you. Place a green candle in a holder there, and put the twigs, feathers, and leaves into a silver-plated bowl. Add to them a stone that signifies the Goddess. Then say these words out loud:

> Goddess of the Hunt,
> Goddess of the Moon,
> Send me your power
> In every waking hour.

Whenever you leave home for work or play, stop in front of the candle and bowl to repeat the spell out loud. Memorize the chant, and say it often wherever you are.

The symbols of the Goddesses of the Hunt are the bow and arrow, the crescent moon, the deer, the woods, the horse, magical weapons, perfumes, sandals. When invoking the Goddesses in ritual or in daily life, use the following tools: *stones*—moonstone, moss agate, pink tourmaline, petrified wood; *herbs*—star anise, lily, mushroom, ash, acorn, rowanwood, oak leaf; *oils*—pine, sandalwood, styrax; *metals*—pewter, steel, iron; *colors*—all greens, russet, brown, orange, teal blue; *jewelry/amulet*—a silver claw grasping a crystal.

Goddesses of Wisdom and Crafts

REALMS

Goddesses of Wisdom and Crafts govern all forms of learning and skilled work. They are the rulers of handicrafts such as weaving, sculpture, jewelry making, pottery, music and the arts. The Goddess of Wisdom is the muse for all forms of schooling, training, and educational activities. Some Goddesses

reflect the innate wisdom arising from a deep, intuitive understanding of nature, while others rule over skills and handicrafts
learned only through formal apprenticeship and much practice.
This tribe of Goddesses includes Athene, Brigit, Cerridwen, Isis,
Sophia, Minerva, Arachne, and Blodewedd.

LOVERS

Women ruled by Goddesses of Wisdom and Crafts are
noted for common sense and moderation. They tend to be either introverted in their dedication to solitary handicraft work
and scholarly studies or extroverted to assure their plans are
fully executed. They are enthusiastic planners in the domestic
sphere, large organizations, or careers. They appreciate mentor
relationships, playing the role of either mentor or protégée. Inspired by these Goddesses, a woman will make a good personal
assistant for someone in authority. She will enjoy being an important companion or partner in some skilled or learned enterprise.

If you are attracted to Goddesses of Wisdom and Crafts and
come under their influence, you will probably fall in love with
the head rather than the heart. You may tend to be out of touch
with your body and may not come across as very earthy, sensual, or sexy. You don't seem to mind periods of celibacy. You
may view sex as recreational, but will probably be very good at
it (remember, you have skills!). There is a tendency to gravitate
toward powerful, competent men, and to expect your husband
to be competent at whatever he does. You admire heroic qualities in men and other women. If you are a lesbian, you probably
go for a lover ruled by these same Goddesses.

RITUAL

Invoke the Goddesses of Wisdom and Crafts to increase a love of learning and strengthen the commitment to become skilled or knowledgeable in your field of work. Many women in our society are often not encouraged to pursue higher studies or go into careers requiring the kind of knowledge and training traditionally reserved for men, so women entering these fields can draw upon the strength of the Goddess and make her rituals part of their lives. Especially important: to weave the thread of career into the total cloth of one's life, especially in matters of love and relationship. We can invoke the Goddesses of Wisdom and Crafts to inspire our love life, even as they help us with career or hobby.

For this ritual, you will need to set up a shrine to the Goddesses of Wisdom and Crafts. Ideally, it should be in your office, study, or workroom, but a corner of the bedroom or any other room will be fine. You will need a piece of handicraft, a book, and a mirror. The handicraft might be in any medium that appeals to you or the medium in which you work if you are a craftsperson. It could be a small painting, a piece of sculpture, ceramic figure, pot, or basket containing some image of the Goddess or another inspiring female figure. Select a book, preferably one written by a woman or one who has inspired you at some point in your life.

Set the artwork on the book and position an attractive mirror behind them so you can see the Goddess figure and the book reflected in the mirror, preferably from where you sit to work. Doubling the image of the artwork and book is the objective, symbolically duplicating or increasing the Goddess's skills and wisdom in your own life. When you begin work or whenever you are in the room, invoke the Goddess, saying, "Mother of Crafts, Goddess of Wisdom (or name specific deity), reflect your ancient knowledge in my life. Let my life duplicate the gifts of wisdom and learning you bring to us, and may my own wisdom and skill shine forth to illuminate the lives of others (or name lover) and bring them joy and happiness."

You might also light a candle or burn incense in front of the shrine at appropriate times.

The sacred objects of the Goddesses of Wisdom and Crafts include cauldrons, the owl, the spider, helmet, spear, and shield, eternal flames and lamps. When invoking these Goddesses in ritual or in daily life, use the following tools: *stones*—holy stone, carnelian, malachite, yellow citrine; *herbs*—lovage, mistletoe, sunflower, rue, Saint-John's-wort, marigold; *oils*—styrax, patchouli, heliotrope, heather; *metal*—iron, brass, silver; *colors*—yellow-green, red, blue, gold; *jewelry/amulet*—magic mirror, small basket.

Hearth Goddesses

REALMS

Goddesses of the Hearth are the rulers of the household, the Goddesses of Motherhood and Child-rearing. Their realms are the hearth, the kitchen, the family unit, the home. Hearth Goddess females find their greatest fulfillment in marriage and view being a wife as their primary vocation. These Goddesses choose most of their followers from married women and mothers. But, on the ascetic side, these Goddesses protect all consecrated priestesses who substitute the temple for the home, the sacred fires for the hearthside, the altar for the kitchen table. As many religious orders of women express it, the members are "married to the God." Hearth Goddesses include Brigit, Cerridwen, Hestia, Vesta, Frigg, Arianrod, Hathor, Hera, Isis, Nanna, Juno.

LOVERS

Women influenced by Hearth Goddesses enjoy the quiet pleasures of the home or temple. Unassertive, they prefer to remain in the background, making anonymous contributions and deriving satisfaction from maintaining a clean, well-ordered environment. They are task-oriented and appreciate the quick gratification from simple daily chores. They tend not to be rushed or hurried, flowing easily with the natural rhythms and times of specific tasks and duties. They are very centered, inner-oriented women who develop great wisdom concerning the importance and meaning of everyday things.

If these Goddesses play a role in your life, you will probably seek domestic partners who also enjoy the pleasures of the fireside and the kitchen. You prefer men willing to take an active interest in the house and household tasks, and you are often content to divide chores along traditional male–female lines. You probably do not initiate sex, but you enjoy it. However, if your mate is uninterested, you, too, can take it or leave it. For you, sex is like the home: a sanctuary, a place where you feel good, protected, warm, and safe. As a lesbian, you will enjoy the close bonding from sharing a household with another woman, more than from sexual intimacy with her.

RITUAL

Hearth Goddesses can be invoked by women naturally drawn to household occupations to consecrate that work more fully, or by women who find domestic work unappealing to gain more satisfaction from it.

One of the most powerful tools in Witchcraft is the wand. When used regularly it becomes infused with magical power and energy. The ancient folk notion that waving a magic wand will produce the unexpected is based on the fact that the tool becomes a highly charged, ready dispenser of magic. A wand should not be waved lightly or frivolously. Any long, linear object can serve as a wand. During the years of persecution, Witches were forced to conceal magical tools around the house. Broomsticks, wooden spoons, and kitchen knives were consecrated and used for magic, and when they weren't being used in a spell or ritual, they disappeared into the normal household clutter.

For this ritual, buy a special wooden spoon, the type used for baking or tossing salads. Make a definite quest to find this spoon, preferably in an antiques or secondhand store. Older utensils often feel better in the hand, and they come steeped in years of service. Carve into the handle any sacred symbols or words that appeal to you: the name of the Goddess, your name, the names of members of your family, your lover's name. Charge the spoon to neutralize any energies inappropriate for your household and put into it your own energy and that of the Goddess.

Invoke the Goddess of the Hearth, saying, "Mother of the Hearthside, Goddess of Home and Family (or name specific Goddess), charge this spoon to become a magical tool for my purposes, so it will channel into my work your love and compassion. By this act, I make this humble object a tool of power and magic. I name it Wand of the Goddess."

Hang your wand on the wall or keep it wrapped in special linen in a drawer apart from your other kitchen utensils. It should not be used as just another spoon, except ritually to stir magical soups, sauces, and other dishes. When you do, take it from its special place and intentionally use it to transfer into the food the power of the Goddess and your own love and compassion. Say, "With this wand I stir into this dish (name it) strength, love, health, and joy. I prepare this meal for (name mate or family members) so that it will nourish the spirit even as it nourishes the body."

Symbols of the Hearth Goddesses are the hearth, sacred fires, the home, the temple, altars, cauldrons, the larder, the pantry, the closet. When invoking these Goddesses in ritual or in daily life, use the following tools: *stones*—fire opal, rhodochrosite, smoky quartz, garnet, ruby; *herbs*—benzoin, broom, coriander, dragon's blood resin; *oils*—hyssop, honeysuckle, wisteria, vertiver; *metals*—gold, brass, bronze; *colors*—pink, red, orange, rose; *jewelry/amulet*—miniature silver cauldron worn as a pendant, small black cauldron for the stove.

Goddesses of Fertility

REALMS

This cluster of Goddesses includes the classic Fertility Goddesses and Earth Mothers such as Demeter, Ceres, Isis, Freya, Astarte, Inanna/Ishtar, Cerridwen, Una, Nerthus, and Epona. These Mother Goddesses rule over the fertile Earth itself and each individual field plowed, planted, and harvested. They protect all phases of conception, birth, life, death, and rebirth. They represent the Great Womb of life and into their bodies all living things return for they are also the Great Tomb. In life, they are the great providers and nurturers. They nourish the maternal instinct in women and teach the mysteries of menstruation.

LOVERS

Fertility Goddesses are solid, reliable deities with their "feet on the ground," so to speak, and so are the women they influence. They tend to be generous, warm, giving, practical, commonsensical mother figures, loyal to family and deriving great satisfaction in doing for others. On the darker side, the Great Mother can become the Devouring Mother (such as the Goddess Kali) who consumes her children. If not held in moderation, their need to "mother" others can do great harm. It can suffocate children and stifle their unique personalities. And yet, women ruled by these Goddesses have a deep understanding of death-in-life and life-in-death that lies at the heart of fertility. More than Hearth Goddesses, Fertility Goddesses can assist women in appreciating the cyclic nature of existence in its broadest scope: from womb to tomb.

If a Fertility Goddess is active in your psyche, you respond easily to men and their advances since your maternal, procreative drive is strong. You can be greatly attracted to men you can mother, replicating the classic Goddesses who mated with their Son-Consorts. Men attracted to you may be living out the old song lyrics about finding a "girl just like the girl who married dear old dad." In general, you prefer family men who will be good fathers and loyal husbands. Once you become a mother, your sex drive may not be strong. You may even be somewhat puritanical, since your greatest enjoyment comes from simple cuddling and nonsexual displays of affection, similar to the way you nurture children. You use sex for procreation or for nurturing and pleasing a husband.

RITUAL

Rituals for Fertility Goddesses should invoke that special wisdom of uniting life and death. We invoke these Goddesses to deepen our understanding that nothing lasts forever and that life moves in cycles. In times of sorrow or loss, the Goddess reminds us that giving away is as important as acquiring things. In fact, nothing is ours to keep forever. Everything must be returned after we use it. Such is the law of nature.

It is an old custom among Witches to bake special cakes or cookies in honor of the Goddess. These are then used in coven circles or left outside at sites that are sacred to the Goddess. Here is a recipe for honey cakes:

2/3 cup shortening
1 cup sugar
2 eggs
1 1/2 teaspoons honey
1 teaspoon vanilla
1 teaspoon white wine
1 teaspoon of herbs or spice for your intention
2 1/2 cups flour
1 teaspoon baking powder
1 teaspoon salt
2 tablespoons oats

Mix shortening, sugar, eggs, honey, vanilla, and wine. Then add herbs or spice. Blend in baking powder, flour, salt, and oats. Mix together. Spoon batter onto cookie sheet. Or roll out and cut in the shape of a crescent moon. Bake at 350 degrees for 9 or 10 minutes.

This ritual can be done at any time of the month, but we encourage you to do it under the full moon. Take a cake and a chalice of wine. Go outside and offer them to the Goddess in her Full Moon aspect, the Great Mother. Say, "I call upon you, Great Mother (or name a specific Goddess), to watch my rite. I take this cake and wine. Here are your grains and your grapes, transformed by human hands, even my hands, into food and drink." As you say these words let the moon's light shine into the chalice and shimmer on the wine.

Then dip the cake into the wine and take a bite of it. Pass the chalice and cake to others if you are doing this ritual with friends. When everyone has taken a bite, a small piece should remain. Offer this last piece of cake to the Goddess in the Moon, and crumble it into the remaining wine. Again raise the cup to the moon, and then reverently pour it out onto the earth.

Before you leave, say, "From the Earth come food and drink, and into the Earth they return, as do we, as do all living things. Blessed be the Great Mother."

If you are doing this ritual because of some sorrow or loss, you can say, "I pour this wine and cake back into the Earth, even as I let go of (name your sorrow or loss). Nothing is mine forever, all things are Hers. The gifts are simply ours to borrow. And now I return them."

The symbols of the Goddesses of Fertility include sheaves of wheat, barley, corn, sunflowers, the Full Moon, the cow, the snake. When invoking these Goddesses in ritual or in daily life, use the following tools: *stones*—topaz, geode, tourmaline, clear quartz; *herbs*—holly, moonwort, rosemary, orris root, ash, pumpkin, samiana; *oils*—rose, poppy, primrose, strawberry, violet; *metals*—gold, brass; *colors*—red, rose, pink, peach, ivory, green, black, dark brown, wheat colors; *jewelry/amulet*—crystal or silver crescent moon.

Goddesses of the Deep Earth

REALMS

Goddesses of the Deep Earth are the Queens of the Underworld, strong Otherworld Spirits, and the Goddesses of Wells, Lakes, and Rivers. Some of them are the primordial Goddess figures who created or cocreated the Universe. They include Persephone, Hel, Gaea, Tiamat, Circe, Coventina, Cybele, Vivienne, Nimue, Rhiannon, Rhea, and Sulla. These are the Goddesses of magic, mystery, and deep instinctual knowledge, and some serve as guides to the Lower Worlds or the Land of the Dead. Their haunts include caves and caverns, the deep reaches of outer space, and the dark side of the moon.

LOVERS

Goddesses of the Deep Earth can put women in touch with the deep unconscious. Memories, powerful feelings, and dreams are important to them. More than other women's, their lives seem driven by the great archetypal motifs. Like Persephone, they can be held captive by these underworld, unconscious powers stirring within them. They enjoy the role of counselor, friend, guide, and instructor. Many women touched by these Goddesses have psychic powers and make good healers and channelers.

If a Goddess of the Deep Earth rules in your life, you can be extremely passionate, erotic, and orgiastic in sexual encounters. Remember that when some of these Goddesses mated with a God, their union generated the entire Universe. With these Goddesses on your side, you may prefer men who are serious, deep, and show some rapport with their own unconscious, or you may be attracted to easygoing, fun-loving men who can draw you out of yourself. As a Deep-Earth woman, your soul is finely tuned to instinctual knowledge and wisdom, and you can play the muse for a man seeking inspiration from realms beyond or beneath his natural ken.

RITUAL

Call upon the Goddesses of the Deep Earth when you feel the need to get in touch with and trust your deep instinctual feelings or when life contradicts these feelings. The Goddess can give you courage to be strong in showing such feelings to others, especially to your lovers. She can be invoked when you must trust your intuition or when others disparage the insights derived from your inner knowing.

The ideal place to invoke the Goddesses of the Deep Earth is a well, spring, cave, or large lake. If you live in the country, you most likely know where such a place can be found. If you are a city dweller, you may have to substitute a pond or fountain in a park or civic plaza.

If you are drawn to doing "mall magic" as we explained it in Chapter 1, you could do a version of this ritual at the artificial pool or fountain that are now standard features in the more luxurious malls. All material phenomena, whether "natural" or "artificial," are symbols of the Goddess. She is always behind, over, and within the elements of creation. Some magic-workers and shamans argue that anything domesticated or artificial lacks the wildness and instinctual wisdom of nature, and consequently cannot be used for magic or divination. This may be true to some extent. But replicas of natural fountains and waterfalls, as well as domesticated animals, can serve as focal points for altering your state of consciousness wherein the real magic and transformation take place.

Do this ritual at the dark of the moon to align yourself with the hiddenness of these Goddesses. When the night is darkest we find rapport with the Lady of the Interior Earth and the Maiden of the Wells, for she is acquainted with the dark womb where seeds grow, the dark regions of the earth where the oldest mysteries dwell.

For this ritual you will need either some coins, seeds, or flower petals. It is an old Celtic custom to toss coins into wells or springs as an offering to the spirits who dwell there. (This may be the origin of the "wishing well" custom of tossing a coin to make a wish.) It is not crass capitalism to use money for magic. Coins are a form of metal, which comes from the earth. They also represent power. For both these reasons, they make a fitting offering. Seeds are the source of life and nourishment. Tossing some onto the water to be carried off in the current is a form of sacrifice, surrendering your claim to them in appreciation for the seeds you plant. Strewing flower petals on the water expresses gratitude for the pleasure they have brought you.

Take your offerings and bless them the night before the ritual, and place them somewhere near your bed. If possible, incubate a dream dealing with your needs or Goddess imagery. An easy way to do this: As you go to bed and place your offering nearby, state that you will accept whatever you dream as a dream-gift from the Goddess. In the morning, interpret the dream along the lines of your intentions. No matter the content of the dream, you will find meaning and significance in it.

The next day take your offering to the well or spring, and toss it in. Say, "Goddess of the Deep Earth (or name a specific deity), let your wisdom flow from the depths this water represents. Let it flow through me, and may I be a channel of deep love and joy for others. I offer you these tokens over which I have dreamed. Accept them as a sign of my dedication to you and the knowledge and power you bestow."

The symbols of the Goddesses of the Deep Earth are the bat, the owl, the wolf, the nightshade plants, pomegranate, willows, crystals, wells, waterfalls, seashells, cauldrons. When invoking these Goddesses in ritual or in daily life, use the following tools: *stones*—slate, marble, hematite, amber, sandstone, boji stones, brown diamond; *herbs*—mastic, adam-and-eve root, ginseng, motherwort, oak moss, mandrake root; *oils*—patchouli, frankincense, myrrh, styrax; *metals*—iron, bronze; *colors*—beige, brown, gray, rust, black, indigo; *jewelry/amulet*—black obsidian, jasper.

Goddesses of Love and Beauty

REALMS

The classic realms of these Goddesses cover all matters pertaining to love, beauty, and seduction. These Goddesses inspire men to fall in love, usually for physical reasons. As Goddesses of Glamor and Sexual Enchantment, they are the primeval models for our concepts of physical feminine beauty. Over the years they have gotten a bad rap for being frivolous and shallow (analogous to the "dumb blonde"), but their true strengths come from a knowledge of love and sex appeal. The classic Goddesses of Love and Beauty include Aphrodite, Venus, Isis, Grainne, Inanna/Ishtar, Astarte, Blodewedd.

LOVERS

Women influenced by Goddesses of Love and Beauty enjoy falling in love and making love. Physically they radiate sex appeal. When they walk into a room they turn others' heads. The mysteries and rituals of love are their domain, and they can spend a great deal of time, perhaps more than most people, plotting and planning their affairs. Extremely creative in relationships, they may feel compelled to continually find new ways to satisfy their strong physical and emotional needs. Often misunderstood as frivolous and shallow, women ruled by these Goddesses may have to go extra lengths to prove their beauty is more than just skin-deep.

You may experience a Love Goddess's influence most intensely during ovulation, fourteen days before menstruation. But whenever she enters your life, you may be extremely driven by sexual needs. Your strong earthy instincts can be wonderfully erotic and sensual. You tend to appreciate all sensory experience: touch, taste, smell, and sight. Sometimes you fall for men who are not good for you, men who are too moody, volatile, or immature. Men who easily fall in love with love can fall for you. As a mortal Love Goddess, you are not content with long-lasting, monogamous relationships. You grow tired of just one companion and may prefer a series of lovers.

RITUAL

Goddesses of Love and Beauty can be invoked to feel more confident about your own natural beauty or to overcome the notion that a woman who enjoys pleasing men is somehow a temptress or harlot. The conservative religious influence in our society causes many women to feel guilty about being seductive, even about spending too much time on personal appearance. The Goddesses of Love help overcome those guilt feelings. Their rituals can add a sacred dimension to bathing and grooming routines.

Select a specific Goddess of Love who appeals to you for some personal reason. Buy your favorite candies. Put clean sheets on the bed.

On the new or full moon, prepare a hot bath with one drop of rose oil, ten drops of patchouli, and one teaspoon of sea salt. Light as many pink candles around the tub as you wish (you cannot be too extravagant). Turn on soothing, magical music. Slip into the tub, and sprinkle dried rose petals on the surface of the water. Take a long, leisurely bath, get out, and wrap yourself in a special pink towel used only for ritual baths. Then slip into some sheer or silky gown (pink, black, or white) or wrap a fancy sheet around you. Stand in front of a full-length mirror, or tilt one so you can see your entire body. Place a few of the pink candles between you and the mirror. Drop your gown or sheet, and observe your body in the soft candlelight. Run your hands over your body, admire the physical charms and assets the Goddess has given you. Envision the Goddess within your body, for she is within everyone, and will now be even more evident in your own.

Say out loud:

> *I am the Goddess of Love.*
> *I am love itself.*
> *Love belongs to me,*
> *Love that is sweet,*
> *Love lasting long,*
> *Love sweet to eat.*

Eat one of the candies, and watch yourself in the mirror indulge in the sweetness of the treat. Repeat the chant as many times as you wish. Place one piece of candy under your pillow to bring you sweet dreams of love, lust, and sexual abandon.

Variation:

Buy new cosmetics: base, powder, blush, lipstick, eye makeup, moisturizer, and so on.

Place a rose quartz crystal in your jar of moisturizer.

On a new moon, take a ritual bath (as above), complete with the mirror, candy, and chant. Then put on makeup for a night out, dressed in your most seductive outfit.

The special symbols of the Goddesses of Love and Beauty are springtime, roses, lilies, violets, clover, gardens, cosmetics, perfume. When invoking these Goddesses in ritual or in daily life, use the following tools: *stones*—rose quartz, pink calcite, green calcite, rhodochrosite, moonstone, emerald; *herbs*—lovage, yarrow, hibiscus, willow, roses, apple; *oils*—rose, patchouli, violet, yarrow, strawberry, vanilla; *metals*—silver, gold; *colors*—light lavender, pink, mint green, white, black, purple; *jewelry/amulet*—heart or apple pendant.

Goddesses of Sovereignty

REALMS

Goddesses of Sovereignty include Warrior Goddesses and the classic Goddesses of the Land, such as Dana, Epona, Brigit, Macha, Scathach, Medbh, Morgain, the Morrigan, Ishtar, Athene, the Amazons, and the Valkyries. Some are the chief lawgivers of their people. Often they are the patron deities of particular cities or tribes and ritually mate with the king or primary male chieftain. They unleash war, preside over battles, and gather dead warriors from the field and lead them into the Otherworld. As Goddess of the Land, they rule over the earth's bounty.

LOVERS

Powerful queenly and priestly figures, Goddesses of Sovereignty demand service, loyalty, and patriotism. Women influenced by them can be devoted matriarchs of their families. They make excellent strategists who have the ability to empower and inspire others—children, siblings, friends, lovers—to perform great deeds. Like the Goddess, these women may be patrons of the arts or sciences. Independent and controlling, they sometimes challenge their heroes in order to test their mettle and keep them humble. Nations and families may fall, but these women endure. Persisting through time as the bedrock of a family's history, they become symbols of constancy.

When a Goddess of Sovereignty governs your life, you tend to demand a great deal of autonomy and expect to receive your due. You look for mates who will honor you in some public way, deferring to your needs and interests. You can be dominant, controlling, sometimes with a strong temper. On the other hand, yours is the art of negotiating and playing fair. You are a power lover who enjoys taking the initiative and calling the shots. With another dominant, controlling person, you may find it hard to compromise differences.

RITUAL

Goddesses of Sovereignty are invoked to empower oneself and gain self-confidence. Women who enjoy playing the queenly or priestly role will do well to be guided by these powerful deities. They can also temper strong, dominating personalities.

The heart of this ritual is a bath, prepared and taken in the most luxurious manner possible. Some suggestions: candlelight or an oil lamp, incense, bath oils or bubbles, soft music, a glass of wine, a special towel, preferably in royal purple or with some courtly design, an enormous and incredibly soft sponge, a special bar of soap (preferably expensive and exquisitely scented), a small statue of the Goddess placed on the rim of the tub or somewhere in view while you are bathing. Needless to say, we suggest you purchase all these accessories especially for the ritual, and use them only in ritual baths to invoke the Goddess. Charge the accessories sometime before the hour of the bath, so they are ready when you are. Keep them in a special place.

The best time for the ritual bath is at night and when you are alone in the house and will not be disturbed. Draw the bath water hot and steamy. Steam and mist have always been associated with the Faerie folk and that land "betwixt and between" the two worlds. In Celtic lore, mist is the breath of the Dragon that represents the Earth Goddess, the primal serpentine energy of the globe. Make the water as hot as you can stand it to simulate a steam-bath or sweat-lodge atmosphere.

Slip into the tub, offer the wine to the Goddess and take a sip, then pour a small amount into the water. Snuggle down under the water as far as possible and relax. At some point, become aware of your complete control of the environment and how it has been arranged to please only you, to serve your needs and no one else's. Luxuriate in the feeling of sovereignty. Reflect on the watery world as a kind of womb, like yours, like your mother's, like her mother's before her, going back to the Great Goddess who birthed the universe into existence from her own divine womb. You share that power and honor with all women. You are a Goddess.

Let your consciousness sink into these primordial feelings of power, enjoy the sense of control, of being a priestess of the water. At some point, when it feels right, invoke the Goddess with words like: "Mother of Sovereignty, Lady of the Land, Goddess of the People, you are the Mother of Tribes, you are the law of nature. Let my powers reflect your own. Give me confidence to (state your goals). Teach me your special wisdom, your clarity to know what to do in all situations (or name a special area)."

For a purification ritual after overstepping your power or being too demanding with your lover, change the invocation to express your sentiments, and ritually bathe your body to wash away the excesses that cause trouble in your relationship.

When you emerge from the bath, take extra time drying off, and if possible go immediately to bed, and ask the Goddess for a dream to provide insight into your role as her daughter.

The symbols of the Goddesses of Sovereignty include the sword, spear, shield, ravens, crows, birds of prey, lamps, throne, crowns, scepters, battle cries. When invoking these Goddesses in ritual or in daily life, use the following tools: *stones*—a stone from a castle, a stone beaten by the sea, moss agate, tree agate, aventurine; *herbs*—ivy, moss, oak bark, cohosh, laurel leaves, cedar, lemon grass, milkweed, datura; *oils*—musk, opium, civet, lavender, heather, pine; *metals*—steel, iron; *colors*—turquoise, indigo, all greens, gold, silver, plaids; *jewelry/amulet*—silver/gold bird or sword, miniature magic wand or scepter, metalic fabrics.

Goddesses of the Night

REALMS

Goddesses of the Night rule the Otherworld, the Land of the Dead, the Dark of the Moon. They are the Crone Goddesses, the elder wise women, acquainted with the night and the things of night: aging, decay, death. They are the Grandmothers, the ancient ancestors of the tribe, steeped in a wisdom broader and deeper than intellectual knowledge or practical skills. In their youth, they may have been Huntresses, Warriors, Crafters, but now their interests are more eternal, less concerned with the things of earth. Among these Goddesses are Rhiannon, Hecate, Kali, Dana, the Banshees, and the Morrigan.

LOVERS

Women ruled by Goddesses of the Night are wise, compassionate, unsentimental counselors. They play the roles of elder sister, grandmother, baby-sitter, chaperon. Not caught up in the passions and fads of the moment, they seem aloof to current events. Detached from people, events, prestige, and power, their identities and self-worth are not tied to external circumstances. They have seen everything or give the impression they have. Their strong spirits have been tested by the fires of life. Their memories are long, and they enjoy the role of storyteller and keeper of the folk memory.

As an older woman, you can have a strong and fulfilling love life as a wiser, calmer version of your youth. You are now more patient, understanding, and accepting of others. Clearly, you need a mate who appreciates your special needs and the special role you play at this stage in your life. On the other hand, you may have grown beyond sex and partnership altogether to be an independent, free agent who can be many things to many different people.

Ritual

You don't need to be in the Crone stage of life to invoke the Goddess of the Night. Her wisdom and counsel is helpful to women of every age. Her great gift is the ability to put things in perspective, to take the long view and see current predicaments against an eternal backdrop. As Grandmother Spider she sees the entire web, having woven much of it herself. She can help you find your current place on it and suggest directions for the future.

If you are an elder, a widow, or facing death, let the Goddess draw you into her orbit, and strengthen and comfort you through this important phase of your life.

Do the ritual at the dark or waning moon. The most auspicious time is midnight. You will want to bake a special honey cake for the ritual. Here is a suggested recipe.

2/3 cup shortening
1 cup sugar
2 eggs
1 1/2 tablespoons honey
1 teaspoon vanilla
1 teaspoon white wine
2 1/2 cups flour
1 teaspoon baking powder
1 teaspoon salt
2 tablespoons oats

1 teaspoon herb or spice of your choice for your intention

Mix shortening, sugar, eggs, honey, vanilla, wine, and the
herb or spice of your choice. Then blend in baking powder,
flour, salt, and oats. Mix very well. Spoon onto a greased cookie
sheet in small circles. Or roll the mixture out and cut moon
shapes. With your athame (or kitchen knife), etch pentacles in
them. Cook at 350 degrees for 9 or 10 minutes.

If you cannot bake a cake for whatever reason, buy a simple
pound cake at your local bakery (not a prepackaged cake).
You will also need a "Black Moon" oil. Here is a recipe.

1 dram orchid or almond oil
1 dram vanilla oleo resin
1 dram vetiver oil
Mix all three together.

These oils are becoming more readily available in botanical
and herbal shops. If you cannot get all three, any one will
suffice. (Note: These oils are to be worn, not eaten or imbibed.)
Traditionally Witches leave cakes for the Morrigan, the Goddess of the Night and the Crossroads, at a spot where two roads
or paths cross. In Salem we use the center of the Salem Com-
mons, where several paths intersect. You can find crossroads in
local parks or plazas. If you live in an area where it is not safe to
go alone, take a friend. If the neighborhood is truly dangerous,
then make a crossroads in your own yard with poppy seeds.
Take two handfuls (one in each hand) and walk the length of
your yard (at least ten paces), strewing one handful of seeds as
you walk. Then walk across this line near the middle for at least

ten paces, dropping the seeds from your other hand. The seeds may not be visible in the grass. No matter. You and the Goddess know they are there.

Begin the ritual in your home at your altar or the place where you groom yourself. Anoint your heart, navel, and forehead with the Black Moon oil. At the heart say, "I am the Goddess of the Hunt, the Maiden of the Woods, the Lady of the Wild things. I follow my heart." At the navel say, "I am the Great Mother, the Goddess of Ripeness and the Fertile Earth. I am the womb of all life." At the forehead say, "I am the Crone of Wisdom, the Keeper of the Gate. I am one acquainted with the night."

Then leave your home and walk to the crossroads with your food offering. As you go say words to the effect: "I go into the night. Goddess of the Dark Moon, walk with me. Give me your strength and your courage. I step along your sacred path. I stop at the place where two roads cross, the place where the worlds intersect. Here is the place of decision, the turning place. I am your daughter, and ask for help to (state your request). Here in your sacred spot of power I leave this token of love."

Leave the food, and perhaps a few drops of the Black Moon Oil, and depart without looking back.

The sacred symbols of the Goddesses of the Night are the torch, crossroads, graveyards, night owl, yew and willow trees, howling dogs. When invoking these Goddesses in ritual or in daily life, use the following tools: *stones*—shale, slate, blue quartz, black coral, obsidian, diamond; *herbs*—willow, oak moss, cedar, foxglove, datura, all night-blooming flowers, garlic; *oils*—opium, musk, civet, neroli, styrax, vanilla; *metals*—silver, platinum; *colors*—indigo, royal blue, purple, silver, black, burgundy; *jewelry/amulet*—claw or tooth set in silver or gold.

Two Supplementary Spells

In addition to the individual spells and rituals for each group of
Gods and Goddesses, the next two spells can be adapted to any
deity. The first locks up any God's or Goddess's positive or
negative energy harmful to you or your relationship for whatever reason, because either it is destructive or just inappropriate, too powerful, too disruptive for the moment. The other is a
libation ritual, to thank a God or Goddess for entering your life
and helping you out in a particular situation.

BINDING SPELL

To neutralize and bottle up any harmful effect of a God's or
Goddess's energy. You will need:

> 4 tablespoons frankincense or myrrh
> 4 tablespoons powdered iron (available at pottery shops
>   where ironstone is made)
> 4 tablespoons sea salt
> 4 tablespoons orris-root powder (or oak moss)
> 1 white candle
> 1 bottle with a cork or lid
> parchment paper
> black ink or black ballpoint pen
> black thread
> a stone, herb, or symbol of the deity whose energy you
>   wish to bind

Mix the sea salt, orris-root powder, and iron in a bowl.
Then cut a piece of parchment to fit inside your bottle and write
on it with black ink, "I neutralize the power of (name deity) to

do any harm to me or anyone (or mention your lover by name). I ask that this be correct and for the good of all. So mote it be."

Roll up the parchment, tie it with a black thread to bind it, and place it in the bottle, along with the stone, herb, or symbol of the deity. Fill the bottle with the dry ingredients. Then take the white candle and, while turning the bottle counterclockwise, drip wax over the cork or lid to seal it. Last, secretly bury the bottle in a place where it will not be disturbed and no animal or person will dig it up.

Another way to bind harmful energy is with a cord spell. Take two 13-inch strands of cord or thread, one white, the other black. Burn incense, and hold the two cords next to each other, as if they were one, in both hands over the smoke. Slowly tie a knot in the middle of the strands while you say, "With this knot I bind the power of (name the deity) to do any harm to me or the ones I love. May this be correct and for the good of all. So mote it be."

LIBATION RITUAL

Sometimes we realize after the fact that a deity was present and influential in our lives: a Trickster God getting us out of a scrape; a War God assisting us in some competitive enterprise; a Love Goddess helping out on a first date; a Goddess of Wisdom and Learning quickening our minds during an exam. Later we want to express our gratitude. Here is a ritual for doing that.

Take a chalice or special cup and fill it with wine, ale, mead, or sweetened springwater. Go outdoors to a sacred spot, a sanctuary garden, or an outdoor altar. (Three upright stones of the same height, arranged in a triangle, with a flat lintel stone placed over them, like a dolmen, make a good libation altar.) Cast a circle by offering the chalice to the four directions and invoking the natural elements and spirits of those directions. Charge the cup and drink within it.

Then raise the chalice to eye level, and say, "I drink this cup for love, health, and prosperity, and I honor the Powers that watch over me. (Take a swallow.) I offer this sacred drink to (name the deity and take another swallow) and to all the Gods and Goddesses of the universe." (Take a third swallow and pour the remainder onto the altar, or into a special place on the ground where no one will walk on it.) Spend a few moments while the ground is still wet and the drink is soaking into the earth. Thank the elements of that place and then leave.

Spells to Attract Love

In "The wooing of Etaine," one of the most beautiful Irish legends of love and romance, Ailill expresses uncontrollable love for Etaine. "My love is a thistle, it is a strength and violent desire, it is like the four quarters of the earth, it is infinite like the heavens: it is closer than the skin, it drowns like a flood, it is a battle against a ghost, it is a race toward the sky, it is a treasure under the sea, it is a passion for an echo."

Love is a truly cosmic emotion, as Ailill describes it, and men and women turn to the magic of the cosmos to draw this mysterious thing called love into their lives. From earliest times, people have used magic to attract lovers. Love spells, charms, philters, and lust-inducing potions were concocted by ancient Persians, Assyrians, Chinese, and Egyptians, some recorded on scrolls of Egyptian papyrus that go back to 2400–1900 B.C.E.

This chapter gathers together spells, old and new, to attract a lover. It is important as you read them, and practice them, to remember the principles of magic discussed in the first chapter: namely, no spell deprives another human being of free will and personal autonomy. Some spells, particularly older ones, are worded to imply that the target of the spell will be helpless against your charms, but we believe this is an archaic way of putting it, more indicative of the magic-worker's wishes than the potency of the magic. As modern Witches, we do not subscribe to coercive magic, that is, spells to *make* someone do your will. As a form of mind control over another human being, this would be, were it possible, invasive and unethical, unless it was done with the full knowledge and consent of the other person.

Frankly, my belief is that magic done for the good of all and with the specific intention to harm no one is inherently noncoercive because it sends out only suggestions and benign influences on a psychic, magical level and the so-called target of the spell can refuse to respond. You are, in effect, saying, "If it is not good for everyone concerned, then I don't want it!"

A physical analogy might be helpful. Consider what might happen if you go up to someone you recently met, and in your sexiest, most seductive voice, you whisper in his or her ear, "I plan to get you in bed by Friday night!" What chutzpah! It just might work! Then again it might not. It could backfire with a response like "Buzz off, sweetheart!" Regardless of your success or failure, it is certainly not unethical to be blunt. Nor does it deprive the other of the power to say no.

Magic spells work in a similar, but less blunt, way. Some people assume, however, that because the magic-worker does not lay his or her desires right out in front of the other person, magic is "sneakier" and therefore not as ethical. It is true that the spell—the "magical come-on"—works on a psychic level, and for that reason it is "occult" or "hidden." But operating on a psychic level does not make a spell unethical, precisely because everyone has psychic radar and can intercept a spell if he or she wishes. In other words, love magic does not deprive a recipient of "psychic autonomy." Everyone can resist psychic influences to a sufficient degree to maintain their independence and self-control. That's why love magic sometimes doesn't work. On a psychic level, your intended is aware of your magic and can decide how to respond—maybe by hopping into bed with you even before Friday night, or by sending you the psychic equivalent of a polite "Get lost, creep!"

Perform the love spells and rituals in an ethical manner, respecting the Goddess who dwells in everyone. Spells are not a means of gaining power over someone else. They should not be done in a spirit implying the other person is any less Goddess- or God-filled than you are. Or any less power-full, for that matter.

We hope your spells are successful and that your love is a thistle, strong as the four quarters, closer than the skin, a treasure under the sea, a race for the sky, infinite like the heavens.

SPELLS TO FIND A LOVER

Moonbath Spell

I always do this spell on a Friday when the moon is full. It is even more powerful if the Friday occurs with the full moon in Taurus. Or it can be done on the third full moon after your birthday, regardless if it is on a Friday. Perform this spell during the three hours before the moon is actually full. Place a full-length mirror (or a mirror tilted so you can see your entire figure in it) near a window where moonlight enters. Take a long, leisurely ritual bath. (Although these ritual baths have been described in Chapter 6 for women, men can adapt them, choosing deities, bath oils, toiletries, and dressing gowns that fit a masculine style.)

Wash your hair, make up your face, dress in a sheer long gown or robe, or wrap yourself in a sheet. Light three candles (silver, white, and light blue). Then stand or sit in front of the mirror. In your mind's eye see the Goddess Venus dwelling in your body. Her beauty permeates your aura. Her love shines out from your eyes. For several minutes, study the various ways her presence manifests in you. Then drop the gown or sheet, and stand naked in the moonlight. Enjoy the sight of your own beauty, for it is the Goddess in you, just as strongly as she is in everyone and everything. Then invoke her beauty with these words, so that others see her in you:

> Goddess of Beauty, Goddess of the Night,
> Mold my body into a beautiful sight.
> Give my hair luster, short or long,
> Give my voice the sound of song,
> Eyes that swallow and drink his love,
> Hands that caress, soft as a dove.

Snuff out the candles to illuminate your body solely by moonlight. See the *you* who are the Goddess of Love and Beauty. Hold that image as you crawl into bed. Allow her to be with you as you fall asleep.

Men can do this spell to invoke the Horned God, and say these words:

> *God of the Wild Things, God of the Wood,*
> *Teach me the ways to quest for the good.*
> *Strengthen my body, deepen my song,*
> *Sharpen my vision, both steadfast and strong.*
> *God of the Wild Things, God of the Dance,*
> *Lead me to love, by design or by chance.*

Love Tea Spell

A love tea can be made on Monday, Tuesday, or Friday during a waxing moon. You will need:

- ◆ three candles (red, pink, and green)
- ◆ 4 caraway seeds
- ◆ 4 fennel seeds
- ◆ 1 tea bag
- ◆ three rose hips
- ◆ five edible rose petals. If you cannot get rose petals, buy rose water or dried roses from a herbal shop. (Be sure that the roses have not been sprayed with pesticides and are safe for brewing into a tea).

Light the candles and place them on the stove near the teapot. Bring two cups of springwater to a slow simmer. Add the other ingredients with the tea. As the love tea is steeping, pass your hands over the steam three times, and concentrate on the feelings of love. Pour a cup and sit in a cheerful place. If you have a photo of an intended lover, place it where you can see it as you drink the tea. Recite this spell:

I lift this cup to my lips,
I drink it slow with tiny sips.
Rose, tea, caraway,
And fennel cause love to stay.

Cat Magic

A Witch often seeks the aid of an animal familiar to help with magic, animal powers being one of the oldest forms of guidance and intuitive wisdom, going back in many cultures to the power animals of tribal shamans. For this spell you will need a little cat fur. If Fudge, Razin, and Louis Vuitton, the three cats who live with me, are at all typical, shedding is one of a cat's great pleasures in life! So just collect some fur the next time you brush off the furniture, or save the fur that sticks to your hand when you pet a cat, or use a steel comb to run through its fur. You can also collect a few whiskers that fall out and keep them for rituals such as this. You should not *cut* any fur off a cat for this spell. Getting clipped is *not* one of the great pleasures in a cat's life.

The spell should be done on a Sunday after a new moon. Before you begin the spell, dress in a special black dress or your ritual robes, groom yourself to look your best, and put on a dab of love potion or cat potion. Sit or stand at your altar or some magical spot in your house. If you live with a cat, bring it into your circle and hold it on your lap. Then say the following words out loud:

Black cat, gray cat, yellow or brown,
Come running through the streets of town,
Meowing, hissing, scratch and claw,

> *Purring happy, remember the law:*
> *To lead and guide me with velvet paw.*

Charge the cat fur and put it in a black-color magic bag or keep it in an envelope (marked so you remember what it is for).

Herbal Smoke Spell

Here is a simple spell, using only an incense burner, instant-light charcoal, and a pinch of dried rose petals or yarrow. Repeat this spell every Tuesday after a new moon and in the hour of Venus, if possible.

When the smoke from the incense rises from the burner, visualize your lover's face in the smoke or the glowing coals. Whisper these words over and over until you feel the magic happening.

> *Magic herbs, burn in fire,*
> *Bring to me my heart's desire.*

Love Box Spell

For this spell you will need:

♦ a special box, one you find beautiful, handsome, stunning, or with some particular charm suggesting romance or a loving relationship. You can use a well-crafted box or a rather plain box you decorate yourself with designs, pictures, colors, and images you associate with love, such as stenciling a heart or a cupid, or gluing lace or jewelry onto it.

- one red, one black candle
- glue

When the moon is new, begin a quest to find love objects for the box. Again, these will be personal symbols of love, sex, romance, or relationship. When you have collected nine objects, charge them to neutralize unwanted energy, and infuse them with your own personal love energy. Place the items and the box on your altar or magic space. Light a red and a black candle. Pick up each object individually in your left hand, and visualize love flowering in your life. Think and feel the strongest thoughts and emotions that you have experienced when you were in love.

Then glue each item into the box so it stays in place. This is an old binding custom to express stability and your desire for a lasting relationship. However, if glue would damage an object, such as your great-grandmother's antique handkerchief, just lay it in the box without glue. Let your feelings guide you as to where to place each object and how to make the final arrangement. If you have a particular person in mind, put his or her picture in the box along with your own.

When you have finished, keep the box in a magical spot in your home. Every now and then, open the box, as you would a treasure chest, letting the energy of the love objects drift upward toward you. You might even waft them up toward your face as you would incense, and inhale deeply, allowing the energy from inside the box to flood your entire body. As you find other objects, charge them and ritually add them to the collection.

Love Totem Spell

The major items you will need are:

- a plant hanger for the ceiling
- enough heavy cord (such as drapery cord) to tie on to the ceiling hook and to knot nine times and still have enough left to lie along the floor
- love potion and love stones

Gather love objects that you can sew or tie to the cord or place on the floor beneath the cord, such as a picture of two famous lovers; a statue of a Goddess or God; dried flowers; an old love letter; love stones such as pink quartz, rhodochrosite, emerald; sprigs of herbs or dried herbs in pouches; Valentines; old wedding invitations; a glass bottle filled with pink or red love powders or glitter; and so on.

Place in front of you all the items you have gathered, go into alpha, and spend a few moments recalling the following romantic adventure as if it had really happened to you in the past or in an earlier life:

The sun is shining on a lush, flowery meadow. Far away on a hill you see a Gothic castle and a romantic pathway leading up to it. You walk through the meadow, along the path, picking flowers and herbs, watching butterflies, listening to the sweet song of birds. A beautiful white horse gallops up to you out of nowhere, nudges your shoulder, inviting you to climb up and go for a ride. You mount the horse bareback, grab the thick, silky mane, and off it runs up the path to the castle. The horse's hooves clop and echo on the drawbridge, and you enter a festive courtyard. Your lover stands in an archway across the yard with arms outstretched, and smiles, so happy to see you. You jump off the horse and run over, throw your arms around each other and embrace with the exquisite intensity of joy, passion, comfort, and unconditional love. These feelings tingle throughout your entire body.

When the power of this memory is strong, tie the first knot in the cord as a loop at the top to hang on the hook. As you tie each succeeding knot, hold the feeling of your lover's embrace in your mind and heart, and see yourself tying that sensation into the cord with each knot. After you have tied nine knots (including the loop), begin to tie or sew onto the cord all the magical objects you have collected. Ones that are too large or heavy to attach can be placed on the floor touching the cord.

Then hang the cord from the ceiling, preferably in your bedroom, and add other objects as they come into your life. You might find them in antiques shops, at garage sales, or out in the wild. The attraction of your love magic will bring them into your life, and you will know them as soon as you see them. Maintaining and developing a love totem will attract love and keep your mind and heart filled with thoughts of love, without which it is hard to be a powerful lover.

Love Budding Spell

It is a custom among many people to force buds in winter by cutting branches of forsythia, bringing them indoors, splitting the stem ends, and putting them in water. The heat and light inside the house "fools" the buds into thinking the longer, warmer days of spring have arrived and it is time to blossom. And so they do! Here is a spell to cause love to bud and blossom during the winter seasons of your life when you have no special person to keep you warm at night.

Anytime after the winter solstice, clip a few branches of forsythia, or other early-budding plants such as flowering quince, winter sweet, witch hazel, pussy willow, weeping willow, or winter cherry. Always prune from below and behind the bush so that you don't take any new growth or ruin the shape of the bush. Bring the branches inside and strike the stem ends firmly with a mallet or hammer to crack the bark and open the cells to draw up water more efficiently. Then place them in a vase of water on your altar. Cast a circle. Charge the branches with your energy. Say the following spell:

> By stem, and by bud,
> By leaf, and by flower,
> Bring me a love
> In the perfect hour.

Recite this spell frequently, and make a strong intention each time that, as the branches bud and flower, love will grow within you and burst forth into others' lives because of you. When we make love flower in others' lives, we open ourselves to receive it in return. Have perfect faith and confidence that the Goddess will send you a lover at the appropriate time, and that he or she will be just the right person for you.

Love Ribbon Magic

My daughter Penny created this love spell with ribbons many years ago. She claims it has never failed to help her find someone. You will need:

♦ three white, pink, or blue ribbons (or one of each color), cut into 9-inch lengths

- ◆ 2 teaspoons powdered dragon's blood resin
- ◆ 1 cup love potion
- ◆ 4 candles (red, pink, white, black)

Mix two teaspoons of dragon's blood resin into a cup of love potion. Light a red, a pink, a white, and a black candle. Sit in a magic circle, and soak the three ribbons in the mixture. Then while they are still wet, or after they have dried, tie a knot in the end of each ribbon while reciting this spell:

> *(on the first ribbon):*
> *Tie one, so shall it be.*
> *Tie two, love will come to me.*
> *(on the second ribbon):*
> *Tie one, the spell's begun.*
> *Tie two, love shall be fun.*
> *(on the third ribbon):*
> *Tie one, the lovers' moon*
> *Tie two, shall bring love soon.*

Wear the ribbons in your hair, or tie them around your wrist or through a belt loop on your jeans, or carry them in your pocket. And be ready! Penny says they work!

Apple Magic

The apple, sacred to Witches, is the magic symbol of love and protection. An old folk custom is to drink apple juice to attract love or to improve your sexual prowess. If you cut an apple through its middle, the five seeds form a perfect pentacle with the red skin of the apple forming the circle. In some places it is believed that if you can peel an apple without breaking the spiraling skin, when it drops to the floor or on the table, it will form the initials of the person who will be your own true love. The custom of eating an apple a day to keep the doctor away began most likely as a love practice. An apple a day brings love to stay!

Another magical practice used by a young girl to determine which of several suitors loved her the most was to take an apple seed for each suitor and toss them one at a time into a fire. The seed that popped—or popped the loudest—indicated the young man whose heart was bursting with love for her.

The apple figures prominently in the tale of the lovers Baile and Ailinn, the Gaelic Romeo and Juliet. The two belonged to feuding royal families, and each died of a broken heart on hearing a report about the death of the other. An apple tree grew out of Ailinn's grave, and each apple on it bore the face of her lover, Baile. From Baile's grave sprang a yew tree that had the appearance of the young girl, Ailinn. Later the two trees were cut down and fashioned into wands, and tragic love songs were inscribed on them.

This apple spell is simple. All it requires is an apple. After every new moon, hold an apple in both hands, and sit or stand where it can absorb the sunlight, or at least pick up the light of day. Cast this spell before you take the first bite.

> *O lovely lady, Goddess of Might,*
> *I honor your beauty and love.*
> *Bring to me a love that is right*
> *Sent by the stars above.*

As you take the first bite, think about the Goddess and the stars above (as well as the five-pointed "seed star" in your hand). Imagine the sweet, moist love-fruit turning into a wild, juicy romance!

Gay Men's Love Spell

John, a young gay Witch, offers this spell, which can be done to strengthen a relation or to attract a particular lover. He warns that as an attraction spell, it has influence only on other gay men. John has tried it on straight men, but it didn't work for him! You will need:

- ◆ coriander
- ◆ dragon's blood
- ◆ mandrake root
- ◆ yarrow
- ◆ one white, one black, and one pink candle
- ◆ love potion
- ◆ parchment
- ◆ incense burner
- ◆ ash pot

Write the following spell on the parchment:

> *Flame of love, burn strong and bright,*
> *Fill his heart with my loving light.*
> *(state your name and your lover's name)*
> *No other man will he see,*
> *With loving arms he will come to me.*
> *So mote it be.*

Blend the herbs while envisioning yourselves in a variety of romantic settings. Carve your name on one side of the pink candle and your lover's on the other. Cast a circle. Then envision yourselves as lovers while anointing the pink candle. Next, burn the herbal mixture as incense, and light the candles in the following order: black, pink, white.

Read the spell out loud, and touch the parchment to each candle flame. Let it burn in the ash pot. As the flame rises say, "In correctness and for the good of all."

Carry the ashes in a black bag or hang it on your bedpost, or bury it where it will not be disturbed.

Sex Stone Magic

People in Celtic countries have always performed fertility rites at certain stones. Especially popular are stones representing the male and female sexual organs. A standing stone, tall and erect, represents the male phallus. A rounded, diamond-shaped, or triangular stone, particularly one with a hole in it, represents the female vulva. Such stones were the objects of pilgrimages by men seeking to renew their virility, young wives hoping to get pregnant, and pregnant women praying for successful and easy childbirths.

Here is a spell to attract a lover, or if you have a lover, to bring him or her closer, and enhance your sex life. Go into the woods or the wooded, rambling area of a park, and look for two stones to represent you and your lover or your hoped-for lover. (Heterosexuals would look for one male and one female stone; same-sex lovers would look for stones of the same sex.)

When you have found two stones (they need not be large), ask for their permission to move them. If they consent, take them to some special place in the woods where they won't be disturbed (or if they are small, bring them home and place them on your altar) and arrange them next to each other, preferably touching, but at least in some recognizable relationship to each other. If one stone is too large to move, or doesn't want to be moved (an obvious interpretation, if it won't budge when you try to pick it up), take the smaller one and bring it to the larger.

Say the following spell after you have united the two stones:

> Stones of Power, Stones of Might,
> Love each other day and night.
> Guard each other in the rain
> Until the sun will shine again.
> Stones of Power, Stones of Might,
> Bring me love if it be right.

Make occasional pilgrimages to the stones. Place your hands on them and draw in their loving energy. Sit or lie on them to allow their power to charge your body. Walk around them sunwise (clockwise) seven times, and recite the spell once each time around. Stones are old and wise. Trust that they will bring you just what you need at this time in your life.

Graffiti Magic

Graffiti is probably as old as human culture. It has only recently become an offensive problem because too many people are scribbling on too many places where too many other people are forced to look at it. Much of it is ugly, permanent, and destructive. But graffiti need not be ugly, permanent, or destructive. It can also be done where it will not offend anyone else. Here is a woodland graffiti spell:

Take a piece of chalk into the woods and draw either the

male and female symbols, or the sun and the crescent moon, on some large, powerful stone or tree, such as an oak, cedar, or birch. We can condone "graffiti magic" because the rain will eventually wash the chalk markings off the stone or tree. They are only temporary and will do no harm. They might even delight an occasional hiker who stumbles upon them before they are washed away. If you go deep enough into the woods, you could actually carve your love symbols on a tree or etch them on stone, where no one else will see them. Love graffiti, when it does not "trash" a natural object or when it will not be offensive to others, really does no harm.

The practice of lovers writing or carving their initials on trees and stone is a very ancient practice. Rock art is one of the oldest forms of human creativity. Almost every ancient culture produced some version of it, and many examples of paleolithic stone art itself concerns fertility in one form or another. As you write your symbols on stone with chalk, feel the presence of your ancestors, who also etched their deepest feelings onto the body of the Great Mother Earth. Your feelings come from the earth, even as they soar into the heavens. As a child of the universe, your feelings of love are cosmic, they can truly unite heaven and earth.

Stone Circle Spell

A Witch friend, April Tuck, created this attraction spell based on her love of old stone circles and the power inherent in the mineral kingdom. You will need:

- ♦ an earthenware dish filled with soil or sand
- ♦ seven small stones from seven different places with special meaning for you

- seven candles: black, white, purple, green, brown, red, silver
- seven earthenware candlestick holders
- a chalice of springwater

On a Friday during a waxing moon, cast a circle and cleanse the above items by holding each in your hand and reciting this charm:

> *Clear, clear, clear you be*
> *Of other intentions save those held by me.*

Take the chalice of springwater and face east, saying,

> *Aisling, Aisling, Aisling,*
> *Bring to this chalice of water pure*
> *The dream talents for a heart so sure.*
> *The one who wishes to drink in your ways*
> *Is the seeker of Love's most powerful rays.*

Take three sips of water, envisioning the Aisling pouring her powers into you through the drink. Dip your finger into the water and place a drop on your heart and a drop on the Third Eye. Set the chalice down between you and the other items.

Pour the soil into the bowl and pat the surface smooth. Pick up each stone individually in your cupped hands and breathe on it to awaken its inner spirit, and say,

> *Small friend, power so old,*
> *Form the ring forged in gold.*
> *Within your circle whisper to me.*

Bring her/him to me.
Say to me that he/she will come.
Summon together with Love's magic fire
The one who should kindle my heart with desire.

After charging each stone, place it firmly in the soil, making a ring counterclockwise. Set the dish on an altar or in a window facing east. Place the candles around the dish in this order: black in the north, then clockwise, purple, red, white, green, silver, brown. Remove the black candle from its holder, hold it, and say:

"Light the path and draw my love to me. Bring him/her now with fire love in his/her heart."

Return the candle to its holder, and do this with each candle in turn. When you have finished, take the chalice and water the stone circle clockwise, making this promise:

I shall water you, awaken you, and let you grow.
I shall nurture you, honor you, and let you sing.
You shall work your magic and your seeds sow.
You shall unite the world and to me my love bring.

Spend a few moments being one with the stone circle, allowing your magic to mingle. Open the circle with a strong word of gratitude to the Aisling. At the new and full moons water the stone garden repeating this chant.

Faerie Love Spell

Here is a magical ritual to call upon the Faerie folk to bring love into your life.

In a magical place outdoors, preferably near a lake or running stream, make a stone circle with sixteen stones or rocks. Make it large enough for you to sit comfortably inside. Sweep the middle for a small altar. Place a ring of flowers just inside the stones. Locate the four directions, and place the following just outside the stones:

+ in the south: a bowl of salt
+ in the north: a pink quartz crystal
+ in the east: two willow limbs
+ in the west: a bowl of springwater

In the center of the circle place an incense burner, then light charcoal and burn dried flowers along with willow, oak, and birch leaves. Sprinkle mistletoe on the ground around the burner. Hold a willow or ash twig in your hand, and sing the following chant:

> *I am a Druid,*
> *I am a Witch,*
> *Faeries, bring me love.*
> *I have a wand,*
> *I have a switch.*
> *Faeries, bring me love.*

Love Spell to the Goddess Aine

Aine is an Irish Moon Goddess who brings luck in love. She is honored at Midsummer, a night when Faeries like to frolic with humans and make mischief. Because she is the Goddess of Good Luck, you can make any intention you wish for this spell, and she will see that it comes true in a correct way for you.

You will need:

♦ dried hay or cornhusks
♦ black string
♦ water or a shovel to put out fire

Tie the hay or cornhusks into a bundle with the black string, arranging them so the end of the bundle can be lit as a smudge stick. Go out into the country or a garden and light the bundle. Let the smoke rise over the flowers or grass and up through the branches of trees toward the stars. Watch the smoke on its journey as it blesses everything it touches. The Goddess Aine will see the smoke. Sit quietly. When she is ready, she will send a procession of Faeries to dance and play around you, beginning the magic to make your love wish come true.

SPELLS TO ATTRACT A SPECIFIC PERSON

Scarlet Love Bundle

On a Friday afternoon, preferably at a waxing moon, gather together

♦ a clover leaf
♦ a rose
♦ three red stones
♦ a red heart (cut from red paper or an old Valentine card)

- one red candle and one pink candle
- a red scarf or a square of red cotton or silk cloth
- thirteen inches of red ribbon.

Place all these items in your bedroom, light the candles on your night table or dresser, lay the red scarf on your bed, and lay the red ribbon aside. Place all the other items on the red scarf. Count into alpha. Visualize your lover or allow an unknown lover to appear in your mind's eye. On the red heart, write these words and speak them aloud three times, addressing them to the God or Goddess whose assistance you are seeking:

> Mix and stir and blend it so
> My lover's heart to wax and grow
> With love for me and great desire,
> The thought of me will thrill like fire.
>   So mote it be.

Gather up all the items in the red scarf and tie it with the red ribbon using three knots. Sleep with this philter under your pillow. Or make two, and carry one with you or keep it in your car. Love philters are one of the most powerful and traditional methods for bringing love into your life.

Love Cake Spell

Here is a love cake you can bake for the man of your dreams.
    For this spell, you need:

- ingredients for a cake
- a pinch of edible dried rose petals

- one teaspoon cinnamon
- springwater set outside or in a window overnight during a full moon.

As you put the ingredients into the cake mix, say:

> A drop of moon blood,
> A pinch of rose,
> Add cinnamon to please his nose.

As you take the cake out of the oven after it has baked, repeat the following spell three times:

> With each bite, we two entwine,
> This spicy cake will make him mine.

Then serve the man you have baked this for a nice, big slice!

Wings-of-Love Spell

The Welsh poet Dafydd ap Gwilym was fond of enticing married women (sometimes nuns!) to tryst with him under a birch, a tree sacred to the Goddess of Love in northern Europe. He lured them to what he called "the religion of the trees and the cuckoo." Often he sent birds as messengers to tell them where or when the next tryst would be. Here is a spell for men, based on this legend.

Collect feathers from a messenger bird, such as a pigeon, gull, crow, or raven. Charge them, and hold them over burning love-incense. Go into alpha, and recite this charm:

Feathers of bird,
Carry my word
Into her heart
Where it'll be heard.

Then shapeshift into a bird and fly out of your home and over to your lover's place. Perch somewhere so you can watch your love, and then sing a verse from any favorite song. When you have finished, fly back home. Then take one of the feathers, wrap it in a sheet of pink or red paper, slip it in an envelope, and mail it to your loved one.

Salted Fire Spell

In southern England young girls used to throw salt onto a fire on three successive Friday nights and recite this rather cruel charm: "It is not this salt that I wish to burn, but the heart of the man I love. . . . May he have no peace nor happiness until he has come and spoken to me." Obviously, this kind of spell gives Witches and other magic-workers a bad name. It is a form of hexing.

But it is the power of a Witch to bend, shape, and change, and we have changed this old folk custom into a more positive spell that will not harm the intended lover, or come back and cause harm for the one who casts it.

Sit in front of a fire, go into alpha, and hold the salt in your left hand. Allow your feelings for the one you love to go into the salt. Just as salt is sprinkled on food to flavor it, visualize your love flavoring the salt. Then toss it into the flames and say: "It is not this fire I wish to salt, but the heart of the man/woman I love. If it is good for both of us, may both our hearts burn with true love for each other. So mote it be."

Fire Jump Spell

It is an old custom in Britain to jump over fires at certain times of the year as a fertility ritual. It can also be part of the Witches' handfasting ceremony. The smoke and heat purify and strengthen one's loins. Obviously, we do not encourage our readers to endanger themselves by leaping over great bonfires. While it's true that firewalking has become popular in recent years, to our knowledge no one is offering fire-leaping workshops (yet), but many modern Witches still celebrate Beltane on May 1 by leaping over a fire.

The custom of fire-leaping can be a powerful, magical rite, and reasonable people can exercise good judgment in deciding the safest way to jump over a fire. The fire need not be large. In fact, for the truly timid (or prudent) a candle will suffice. So would glowing coals from a small campfire. All fire contains the same spirit, and spirit is not a question of size. Fire is fire, heat is heat. The Gods and Goddesses of Fire, Forge, and Hearth dwell in the smallest flame or glowing coal, even as they are in the grandest conflagration.

So light your "fire," then spend a few moments going into alpha, and shifting your consciousness into the purifying and strengthening powers of fire. When you have become fire, begin to dance around the fire, reciting this chant. If you do this ritual with others, the energy will be even more powerful.

> Fire, Fire, burning bright,
> Strengthen me this very night
> To love my love awake, asleep.
> I run to her/him, I fly, I leap!

Repeat the chant and continue dancing until the energy builds. When the moment seems right, time your last verse so you jump across the fire on the words *I leap!* If several people are doing the spell, designate one the dance master who will decide when the energy has built sufficiently to begin the leaping. He or she will then be the first to leap over the fire on the words *I leap.* Each person in turn then recites just the last two lines of the chant before jumping over the fire.

Nine-Day Candle Spell

Here is a nine-day spell to bring a certain person into your orbit, or to attract someone new. You will need one black and one white or pink candle. Begin this spell on a Friday during a waxing moon.

Cast a circle and charge the candles. Draw down the moon and the energies of Venus to empower this spell. Place the candles nine inches apart on your altar, the black candle on the left, the white or pink candle on the right. Light the candles. Visualize the type of person you would like to meet, or someone you already know but would like to draw closer to you. Spend a few moments sending out your energy as a projection for what you want. When the moment feels right, move the white or pink candle one inch to the left, toward the black candle. Visualize the distance between the two flames growing brighter and warmer, and transfer this energy to the distance between you and your lover.

Repeat this for nine consecutive days, preferably at the same time each day, such as in the morning when you get up, or just before going to bed at night. After nine days the candleholders will be touching, signifying the close proximity of your lover. Expect results, and you will get them.

DIVINATION SPELLS

Spinning Basket Spell

Sometimes it is wise to find out ahead of time if you should pursue a certain person you have fallen for. Here is a divination spell from my family's Book of Shadows that will give you a reading on three important aspects of a relationship: fears, sorrows, and how long it will last. You will need:

- three baskets of different sizes
- three candles (brown, green, and pink)
- a bell
- a cord
- love oil or Venus oil

Over a doorway or on a porch, hang each basket from a cord. Anoint the candles with love oil or Venus oil. Light the candles, and sit in front of them and the hanging baskets. Spin the baskets, and repeat this spell:

> *Candles and Wicks,*
> *Wicce and Bell (ring the bell three times),*
> *Soon will cause*
> *A fool to tell.*
> *Baskets hanging*
> *Large to small*
> *Making shadows on the wall.*
> *The first to stop: the amount of fears.*
> *The second tells: the size of my tears.*
> *The third: how long this love in years.*

Note the order in which the baskets stops spinning. Then interpret this order to determine the "fears, tears, and years" inherent in your relationship. Assume that the medium-size basket represents "no more or no less" than what most people experience. In other words, this is what you would perceive as a "normal" relationship. The larger basket indicates you will have "more," the smaller basket indicates "less." Take the message to heart, and tread wisely in your pursuit of this person or back off altogether.

Moonglow Spell

Sometimes we can waste precious time pursuing someone who may break our hearts and our spirits. Here is an omen spell to determine whether a person who is resisting your advances is worth going after.

Write the following magical words on a piece of paper with brown, pink, or green ink.

> *In a forest near the sea*
> *Stands a tall and spreading tree.*
> *I smile at the moon*
> *On bended knee (kneel down)*
> *To learn of love between him/her and me.*
>
> *(Say to the moon):*
> *Gleaming, glowing,*
> *Beaming down.*
> *My heart unsure,*
> *I wear a frown.*
> *Silver for hate,*

> *Golden for love,*
> *Show a circle*
> *Up above.*

On a night when the moon is full, go outdoors, or stand by a window where you can bathe in the moonlight, and recite this spell. As you say the first verse, visualize an apple grove in Avalon, a land sacred to Witches. When you have finished the spell, look up at the moon for an omen. (Note that the love–hate polarity in the spell indicates yes–no respectively; *hate* should not be interpreted to mean that the person literally hates you.) A silver ring or glow around the moon indicates no, that you should not pursue your current love-interest. A golden ring or glow says, "Go for it!"

Acorn Drop Spell

A popular divination spell in olden times that promised to fore-tell whether your lover would be true and eventually marry you used two acorns and a bowl of water. A person would drop two acorns, one representing each lover, into a bowl of water. If the acorns floated next to each other, the relationship would flour-ish. If they floated away from each other, the two lovers would separate and there would be no marriage. If you are not ready for marriage, or your current lover is not marriage material (but you are still madly in love), you can do the spell with the intention of finding out whether you will stay together as lov-ers, rather than to see if you will marry.

I suggest you do this spell in a magic circle, go into alpha, and if the acorns separate, continue the spell to determine how difficult it will be to save the relationship. Here is what to do:

Shift your consciousness into the acorn that "strayed," and
when you have become one with it, move it back psychically
alongside the other, that is, while in acorn-consciousness, guide
and direct it toward the other acorn. If they both seem to have
drifted apart rather equally, shapeshift into either one and guide
it back to the other. If you are not able to do this, you can
conclude one of two things: either your magic is not powerful
enough, or the relationship is not meant to be.

Seed-gathering Spell

In Celtic stories the hero often has to perform some nigh-im-
possible tasks to prove himself worthy of the young woman
who has stolen his heart. A favorite task is for him to collect all
the tiny linseed grains the woman tosses into her yard. This task
is related to a popular divination custom in Celtic lands in
which a young girl scatters linseed or hemp seed in the yard,
and then asks for a vision of her future husband raking or
sweeping it up. This spell was always performed on All Hal-
lows' Eve when apparitions appear quite easily, and if the
woman did it correctly, she would see the shape of her future
husband raking the seed.

Here is a variation of this spell for any time of year. Take a
handful of a tiny seed, such as mustard, linseed, or hemp seed,
to your boyfriend's home and drop a pile of it in a conspicuous,
but not too obvious, place, such as under a table or beside an
easy chair, a place where he is sure to see it. If it looks as if he
isn't going to discover it while you are there, call it to his attention as if you just noticed it. Show some interest it, and get him
talking about why or how it could have appeared out of thin air
so mysteriously. Where did it come from? What does it mean?

Then watch to see what he suggests doing with it. If he sweeps it up and suggests keeping it, either to study it, or try to find out what kind of seed it is or where it came from, your relationship is sound. If he sweeps it up and throws it in the trash, your relationship is on rocky ground and you'd better work harder to strengthen it.

Card Walk Spell

Like many spells in this book, this one too comes from my family's Book of Shadows. In this spell you use the Tarot to divine whether someone currently in your life is destined to become a lover, or whether a new love is soon to arrive. You will need:

- ◆ a Tarot deck
- ◆ a small mirror
- ◆ a magic wand
- ◆ incense (preferably a mixture ruled by Venus)
- ◆ a book of love poems or your Book of Shadows
- ◆ a string of pearls if you are a woman
- ◆ a metal medallion on a leather cord if you are a man

Place the mirror on your altar so you can see your face when you sit before it. Place the incense burner in front of the mirror, and open the book to any page. Close your eyes and go into alpha. Visualize mysterious black clouds flashing with silver lightning. These are not ominous, but friendly clouds, the dragon's breath protecting the Otherworld and you. Shuffle the deck. For women: Visualize a unicorn galloping from the clouds and sitting next to you affectionately. In Western folklore, unicorns had a special affinity for young, inexperienced maidens and protected their pure, chaste energy. For men: Image a white stag leaping from the clouds. In olden love-lore, a stag often showed a hunter the path to his beloved. Another tradition relates that the hunter who killed the white stag could present the magnificent head to the woman of his dreams, thus honoring her as the fairest lady of the court.

Open your eyes, and light the incense. Look at your face in the mirror through the smoke. Hold the pearls or the metal medallion in the smoke and bless them. They represent the power of the Goddess and the God. Then place them around your neck. Shuffle the Tarot cards, and hold the deck in your hands, and repeat this enchantment:

> As black clouds swirl and silver flashes,
> With mirror, wand, smoke, and pearls/cord,
> Open book, and card walk here.
> (Lay the cards down and touch them with the wand.)
> Tell me if my love is near!

Take three cards, place them left to right. Read them to see if someone currently in your life is a lover for you. Then take three more, lay them out, and read them to see if a lover is soon to come into your life. If the answer to both readings is no, then concentrate on doing general spells to bring love into your life.

Spells to Enhance Love

MAY is the lusty month of lovers. This first month of summer in the old Celtic calendar was celebrated by young men and women who went a-Maying, wearing green, braiding flowers and leaves in their hair, enjoying the erotic freedom of the warm season. Traditionally, couples spent the entire night of May Eve in the woods making love and returned in the morning carrying leafy branches as symbols of their night of pleasure. The next day the lovers danced merrily around a birch pole erected in the village square while entwining it with multicolored ribbons.

May was a rebellious month, dedicated to lovers and new romance, not a time for marriage. In fact, a widespread folk belief held that a marriage in May would last only through one summer. Because of this curse on May marriages, lovers waited until June for the wedding that officially sanctioned a relationship begun weeks earlier. Today June is still a favorite month for getting married. But not May—May is for lust, newly discovered love, erotic nights beneath the stars, and extramarital affairs. It is the month of the doe and the wild stag.

This chapter is for lovers. Here you will find spells and love-enhancing rituals to do together, solitary spells to increase your own love or rejuvenate passion in your partner, and protection spells to keep your loved one safe while you are apart.

The Lovers' Branch Spell

In Britain sacred branches with special fruit, nuts, birds, and bells on them played a magical role in the lives of legendary Gods and heroes. For example, bards and poets carried branches, of either silver or gold, that had small bells on them. When they entered a court or festival hall, the music tinkling from the branches announced their arrival and prepared the revelers for the storytelling and songs to come. The famed birds of the Goddess Rhiannon were fond of perching on ghostly trees in the Blessed Islands in the West. The birds' ethereal songs put whoever heard them into a timeless state. In another legend a giant from the Otherworld appeared at Tara in Ireland carrying a branch from a mystical tree laden with nuts, apples, and acorns. Nuts, especially hazelnuts, have a long tradition of bestowing wisdom on whoever eats them. Apples are a love fruit sacred to the Goddess. Acorns are symbolic of the oak, known for its strength and longevity. And the willow represents the Goddess of Love and represents coupling.

We think that this "sacred branch" tradition should be a part of a magical couple's love bower. Although one or the other of the pair can take responsibility for creating the sacred branch, ideally a couple would share the tasks so that the final outcome is a product of their joint effort. For the spell, you will need:

- ♦ a sturdy tree limb that branches out into at least three directions. It should be at least two feet long but can be as long and full as you desire (you can use a branch that has already fallen, or cut a fresh one, but with its permission and in a sacred manner, and be sure to express your gratitude when you have finished)
- ♦ some small bells
- ♦ a small wicker tray or plate
- ♦ an apple, hazelnuts, acorns, and feathers from a songbird
- ♦ a vase or container that will hold the branch in a fairly upright position.

Before the spell, spray-paint the branch either silver or gold —or both, making some branches silver and others gold, silver representing the moon and the feminine, gold representing the masculine sun.

On a night when you intend to make love, gather the items and lay them on the bed. Decide where in the bedroom you will display the arrangement after you have created it, and prepare the place as you see fit. Cast a circle that is as wide as the bedroom. Burn love incense, and light pink and green candles, one on each side of the bed. Get into bed together and sit facing each other, holding hands. Meditate a few moments on your love for each other. Breathe deeply and rhythmically with each other.

When you are ready, take the branch and hold it together, and charge it. Then each of you kiss the branch. Do this with all the other items, one by one: hold the item, either together or passing it back and forth for a few moments, charging it, then kissing it.

As part of the charging ceremony, you might express in your own words to each other, or to the God and Goddess, the following sentiments: The branch represents the tree of life. The tinkling bells and bird feathers bring magical songs that will put you and your lover into a timeless state, a state you wish would go on forever. The apple is the fruit of love. Hazelnuts are to bring wisdom into your relationship. Acorns will make your love for each other strong and enduring.

Fasten the bells and the feathers onto the branch, and place it in the vase or container; then put it in the spot you have prepared. Next arrange the apple, acorns, and nuts on the wicker tray, and place it beneath the branch. Return to bed and make love. When you have finished, put the two candles next to the branch and eat the apple. Then open the circle.

Leave the sacred branch and the tray of nuts and acorns in your bedroom as long as it seems fitting. When you decide to remove it, do so in a sacred manner. Burn the branch, leave the nuts and acorns in the woods or a park for animals, give the bells to children or use them for a decorative purpose.

Love Dance Spell

We know lots of Witches who enjoy erotic dances with their lovers to rekindle their sexual desire for each other. In Salem, Witches love to go to a dance club for an evening of fun and then extend the merriment and the dancing with their partners after they return home in the wee hours of the morning. You can do this anytime, but it works best on a day dedicated to Mars or Venus. Cast a magic circle, anoint each other with love oil, burn love incense, light love candles, put on some kind of stimulating music: either sweet and romantic, or with lusty, sensual drum beats, or exotic belly dancing music. Then dance for each other or with each other. Strip or undress each other as you dance. Continue until you have reached a point of desire that is uncontrollable. Then make love.

Love Poem

Lovers have been writing poetry for ages. Some verses capture the wide range of feelings that accompany falling and being in love and are intended to be seen only by the one who writes them. Others are written specifically to be sent to the lover, usually expressing the poet's undying love. Centuries from now lovers will most likely still become poets, and poems will still sound very much like they always have in the past and the present.

Poetry in shamanic cultures always evokes the other realms, as did the flight of birds, usually associated with the shaman's flight into the Otherworld. It is not surprising, therefore, to discover that Celtic poets wore, as part of their official story-telling clothing, a cloak of bird feathers, and that Druids wore feathers in their headdresses, and that shamans in many cultures use feathers, bird wings, and whistles made of bird bones.

As a magical practice, get in the habit of collecting feathers that you find in the woods or parks, especially feathers from songbirds. Swan feathers are also appropriate. The swan is frequently associated with lovers; and in some folklore traditions, being turned into a swan was an entry into the Otherworld. Feathers of a particularly beautiful color, texture, or sheen are also considered to be meaningful omens. However you see fit, begin a collection of bird feathers to use in spells.

Then the next time you write a poem and send it to your lover, put a few feathers, charged with your love and energy, into the folds of the page before you insert it in an envelope.

I encourage lovers to write poems, even if they do not feel so moved. The experience of expressing your feelings in magical words is powerful, often giving you new insights into yourself, your lover, and your relationship. The easiest kind of verse to write is free verse because you don't need to worry about rhyme or meter or length of line. Your total attention can be focused on the images that reveal the depth and scope of your love.

Here is a very easy method for writing good poetry on the first try. We call it the "catalogue poem." Cataloguing traits and images is not only a good poetic exercise but a method of creating material that can be used as chants. Repeating key images or phrases over and over mesmerizes our attention and prepares the mind to shift consciousness for magical work. A catalogue poem, such as the one below, adapted from a few lines of a Celtic poem written in Christian times to honor a soul friend, can grow out of images from other love poetry. Do not think of this as stealing images from other poets. It is not stealing, but freeing them! Images are meant to live beyond the poem in which they were originally caught. They should become part of the lives and songs of other lovers. You can use this poem as model.

> *My love is pure gold, a heaven around the sun,*
> *A vessel of silver with dark red wine.*
> *My love is a sweet branch with its blossoms,*
> *A jar of honey, a stone found in the creek.*

> *My love is the happiness of summer,*
> *The crispness of autumn,*
> *The stillness of new snow in winter,*
> *My love is the juice and joy of spring.*

You get the idea—images that grab your heart. They'll probably grab your lover's heart as well.

Human Candle Spell

This is Jody Cabot's spell to deepen a relationship of many years or one just beginning. You will need two "human candles," a term that sounds greeblie, but it has nothing to do with setting someone on fire. (*Greeblie* is a Salem word for "macabre.") Human candles are simply small candles made in the shape of human figures. You can buy them in most Witch shops. Or you can make your own. See the instructions following this spell.
   You will need:

- one black candle
- two red candles in the shape of human figures
- one 3-foot black silk cord
- one 3-foot red silk cord
- one plate
- 5 tablespoons coriander
- 3 teaspoons nettle
- 3 teaspoons hibiscus
- love potion
- knife

Write out a list of nine love intentions, such as growth, greater desire, better sex, more attention, more tenderness, more time together, and so forth.

In the hour of Mars on a Mars day, cast a magic circle. Anoint the black candle with the love oil and light it. Place it on the far side of the plate. Anoint the human candles, visualizing you and your lover growing in love for each other. Carve your name in one candle and your lover's name in the other. Lay them on the plate.

Next tie nine knots in the red cord. Speak out loud the nine intentions, one for each knot. Then repeat this with the black cord. Place the two candles so that the figures face each other, and wrap each cord around them and tie it securely. Stand the candles on the plate, and pour the coriander, then the nettles, and last the hibiscus around their base, asking the God and Goddess that this spell be for the good of all.

Light the candles and allow them to burn down. Do this in a safe place away from anything that might catch on fire. Be sure to watch because they burn quickly and the cords might flame up. You can use the melted wax as a talisman.

Make Your Own Human Candle

To make a human candle, take an empty one-quart milk carton and open the top completely. Tie a length of wick or string around the middle of a pencil, and lay the pencil across the top of the carton so the string hangs down inside to the bottom. Pour in wax. When the wax has partially cooled, re-move the candle and carve a human figure out of it.

A Love Growth Spell

This spell comes from Richard and Gypsy, two Salem Witches, who fell in love in a very magical way. They started out as "just good friends" when neither of them had been in a relationship for some time. They made a deal to do magic for each other. Richard created a spell for Gypsy to do; and Gypsy, a song writer, composed a song/spell for Richard called "Wicca Love." They exchanged these spells over the phone, and when Gypsy sang her song, it melted Richard's heart. How could he resist lines like: "Wicca Man, wherever you are/ Will you come from near or far./ Spirit Lover, mate for my soul/ I need you when the Moon is full./ Stay with me and make me whole." Today they are husband and wife and live a magical life together. Here is their spell to increase commitment between partners. You will need:

- two apples
- two pink boxes or two 3-foot love ribbons
- 1 lb. large cloves
- powdered orris root, cinnamon, frankincense, or myrrh

Sit together in a circle, each lover holding one apple. Pin a ribbon into the base of the apple and wrap it around the apple from the bottom to the top. Pin the ribbon securely at the top, leaving enough ribbon to hang the apple, now called a pomander, from a hook or curtain rod. Next stick the cloves into the apple in verticle rows, starting at the stem and proceeding downward to the base. State an intention with each clove. When the apple is filled with cloves, roll it in the spices. Allow the apple to dry in an open bowl for one to two weeks. Then place it in a pink box or hang it in a special room.

The Grail Ritual for Lovers

In Chapter 4 we looked at a ritual done with a cup and blade in which you asked the Grail questions, and we suggested there that if you had a lover, the ritual could be done by both of you together. Here we would like to elaborate on that ritual.

It is important in the Grail myth to ask the questions: Whom does the Grail serve? and Why does the lance bleed? In the context of a relationship, these questions bring up important interpersonal issues, which on a magical level activate the Law of Exchange. All Witches and workers of magic know, as do all human beings on some level of consciousness, that we live in a mutually supportive universe. We cannot just take for ourselves and give nothing back in return. For every deer hunted and slain, for every ear of corn harvested and eaten, for every rainfall, and bright sunny day, some exchange must take place. The universe is and must be balanced. Of all species of life on earth, we humans have the most potential to upset this balance, and we require constant vigilance over our actions, and inactions, to safeguard the greater whole. We must be ever mindful of the "great cosmic swap" and be ready to return something for every gift we receive.

The same is true on the microcosm of a loving relationship. One partner cannot take and give nothing back. The relationship must be balanced by mutual giving and receiving. Occasionally, either through selfishness, or insensitivity to the other's needs, a love affair goes awry, one lover constantly taking, the other giving until there is nothing more to give. The Grail ritual can call this to the lovers' attention, and be the vehicle for correcting the imbalance.

As we have seen, the Grail story is about service and wounds; and in terms of interpersonal dynamics, it is about hurting and healing, giving and taking, joy and sorrow. Both the Grail cup and the lance are within each of us, they are inner mysteries of the psyche. By doing the Grail ritual we develop these sacred power objects through the work of our imagination, building them into consciousness where they work their power on our behalf. We encourage you to ask of yourself every day, or several times a day: Whom does the Grail serve? Why does the lance bleed?

And ask them in your deepest heart where you must be totally honest with yourself. You cannot be in a relationship without hurting your lover. Hurts happen. You and your lover both feel them. Your inner lance bleeds, as does that of your partner. But hopefully the blood drips into the cup and becomes sacred blood, the wine of your relationship, and the life force of your love for each other. The blood is not wasted, the wound is not in vain. Through them you learn, grow, become more loving. And if the cup is filled, it can serve. It can bestow life. It is the cup of infinite blessings enriching your love for each other.

When you lower the blade into the cup and cut a pentacle across the surface of the wine, and every time you see this in your imagination as you go about the business of your day, remember the questions are not about the cup and blade, they are about you. They are about the love of your life.

Candle Magic for Rocky Times

A love candle with oils and herbs hidden in a secret place instills confidence in our power to be good lovers. It is a secret source of inspiration when times are hard and you need to work through problems that arise in your relationship.

Hold a pink candle and charge it for future spells, by visualizing you and your lover in a happy loving embrace. Put the energy from this vision into the candle. Then say out loud, "We will always love each other. May the Goddess and God grant this for the good of all."

When problems arise in your relationship or you need self-confidence, take out the candle on a Friday during a waxing moon and anoint it with love oil using this procedure: Put some oil on your index finger, and beginning in the middle of the candle, run your finger to the wick end. Then repeat, rubbing the oil down to the bottom of the candle. Light the candle and let it burn down completely and go out.

Oak and Ash Spell

This old gypsy spell from England brought back a wayward or missing lover. If a woman found an oak branch with an acorn attached and a piece of ash with its "keys" (the winged seeds in drooping clusters), she put them under her pillow on three successive nights and repeated the following charm:

> *Acorn cup and ashen key,*
> *Bid my true love come to me—*
> *Between moonlight and firelight,*
> *Bring him over the hills tonight;*
> *Over the meadows, over the moor,*
> *Over the rivers, over the sea,*
> *Over the threshold and in at the door.*
> *Acorn cup and ashen key,*
> *Bring my true love back to me.*

After the third night, her lover returned.

The acorn and the ash's key are phallic symbols, so these woods are most suited for a woman's spell. If a man wishes to adapt this spell, we suggest using a birch branch with either a strobile or the cone attached. Change the first and last couplet of the rhyme to: "Birch of the Goddess, with fruit and cone,/ Bring my true love safely home."

Honey Spell

My daughter Jody created this spell to perk up a grumpy lover. Perform it during a waxing moon on a day of Venus. You will need:

♦ one apple
♦ 5 tablespoons honey
♦ one knife
♦ one earthen bowl
♦ one pink candle

Carve your lover's name in the apple and place it in the bowl and pour honey over it. Then chant:

> *Cerridwen grant me my heart's delight,*
> *Make him sweeter night by night.*

Then put the apple in a sacred place, and burn the candle seven nights in a row at 7:00 P.M. for seven minutes. On the seventh night let it burn down. As the flame flickers out, say the chant out loud, adding these two lines:

> *The honey drops from my lips,*
> *He drinks my love in luscious sips.*

Put the honey from the apple on your lips or rub it all over your body before making love.

Love Vows

Lovers always make promises to each other, it is part of being in love. Breaking promises is one of the primary reasons love affairs end. Broken promises, broken love affairs. It seems to be one of the laws of life. Of course, as followers of the Old Ways who watch the eternal return of seasons and the great movements of the Wheel of the Year through landscape and heartscape, we believe that broken promises can be mended, and lovers can make up and carry on, even though reestablishing the trust between the two can be a painful and lengthy process. The Turning of the Year always brings hope.

So what of vows and promises? Is it worth making them? Should they be made in the throes of passion, or coolly and rationally? Should they be bold and forthright, or couched in terms that leave an escape hatch? Each lover will, of course, have to decide for himself or herself. But we do advise thinking about vows and promises in a magical context because the more you consider their impact on your lover, and on you, the more realistic they will be, the less frivolous, and the less chance of breaking them.

We come from a heritage in which the word is powerful, and a pledge of one's faith is not to be taken lightly. The old folk saying that "a man is as good as his word" (and the same applies to women, of course) is no longer accepted as a matter of course. We live in a society that dissembles, "misspeaks," talks in clichés, and creates pleasant-sounding circumlocutions to avoid confronting reality. We speak with forked tongue.

Lovers owe it to each other to speak from the heart, and to be "as good as their word." Trust is the bedrock of a healthy relationship.

The Celtic tribes placed such faith in a person's spoken word, and in a belief in the Afterlife, that it was not uncommon for a person to borrow money on the promise that if it were not repaid in this life, then surely the borrower would do so in the next life. Most Celtic people accepted this. How odd they would find our society where a person's word is not respected, and where people, if they do believe in life after death, see it as some rarified existence totally cut off from the obligations and relationships of this life.

The standard Celtic formula for making a vow invoked the elements as witnesses to the vow and as its executors. It went: "If I break faith with thee, may the skies fall upon me, the seas drown me, and the earth rise up and swallow me." Use this formula with your lover if it expresses your sentiments. This pledge of the elements calls to mind the "triple death," which haunted the Celtic imagination: death by fire (the falling stars); death by water (the raging seas); death by a physical fall (or a fall caused by a creature of earth, such as a stone weapon or metal blade or wooden bludgeon). Each of these three deaths is capable of depriving an individual of the fourth element, air, which is necessary for breath and life. In a deeply elemental way, invoking fire, water, and stone stirs the Gods' and Goddesses' powers manifested in the physical world. The threefold death is the punishment for a broken vow. This is serious business.

I believe that society would be better off if people would be truer to their word, if honesty made a comeback, if men and women lived up to their commitments. I truly believe that relationships between lovers would also be healthier. As a magical practice, find three magazine photos: lightning striking the earth, a turbulent sea, the earth in upheaval or an earthquake fissure. Put them someplace where you will see them, perhaps on your altar or in some nook in your home or office. At odd times, meditate on the power in these elements, or shapeshift consciousness into these elements and experience their titanic force, meet the Gods and Goddesses that reside in them. Then remind yourself that your commitments and promises to your lover should be just as strong and powerful, or . . . or else!

Magical Caption

It can be fun to give a photograph of yourself to your lover with a caption written on it in a magical alphabet. Gypsy gave Richard a photo of herself with the following caption written in the Theban alphabet: "Magician, I am thy Witch." The gift works its spell as the lover translates the caption into our script.

Copper Candle Spell

Jody Cabot and her husband, Harry, do this ritual to strengthen the love in their family. They use:

- three copper candles
- love oil
- a family photo
- rose petals

This simple spell is done on a Friday night just after a new moon. Anoint the candles with love oil and charge them. Arrange the candles as the points of an equilateral triangle, and place the photo in the center. Sprinkle rose petals around the base of each candle. Before you light the candles, speak a spell composed of a few appropriate lines from a favorite love song. Jody and Harry say:

> *You and me and baby make three*
> *How happy we all shall be.*

Then light the candles and allow them to burn down.

Lover's Breastplate

A curious poem has come down to us called "Saint Patrick's Breastplate." There is a Christian hymn that derives from this poem, which begins "I bind unto myself today the strong name of the Trinity." It is an ancient custom to bind to oneself protective powers by drawing down and into oneself the protection of a God or Goddess, the strength inherent in the elements, or the watchful presence of a power animal or spirit guide. If Patrick did in fact write a version of his "breastplate," there is good indication he was building upon more ancient, Druidic spells expressing the same sentiments. Some scholars surmise that Patrick was a transitional figure between the Old Religion and the new Christianity, possibly a former Druid himself, or at least trained in Druidic practices.

You can compose a "breastplate" or "lorica" (from the Latin for metal or leather armor that protected the body from the neck to the waist) for your lover as a protection spell to safeguard him or her when the two of you must be separated for a time. There are several variations of Patrick's lorica. The version below is adapted from one of them. You can use it as is, or as a model to compose your own.

> *I bind unto my love today*
> *The mysteries of the starlit night,*
> *The glorious sun's life-giving rays,*
> *The powers of the moon so bright,*
> *The lightning's magic quick and free,*
> *The whirling wind's tempestuous shocks,*
> *The stable earth, the deep salt sea,*
> *Around the old eternal rocks.*

After you have composed your breastplate, write it out on a piece of parchment, charge and bless it, and give it to your partner before she or he leaves. Or in a magic circle, go into alpha, and say the spell into a special stone that you have selected for this purpose. Bless the stone in air, fire, water, and earth; and then give it to your lover to keep on the trip. Or bind each of the eight elements in this version of the spell into a cord, each with its own knot. Tie the cord around your lover's ankle, wrist, or neck (loosely!) for him or her to wear while apart from you.

Love Doll Spell

Penny Cabot offers this spell to make your partner more loving. You will need:

    a poppet to be stuffed with:
- ♦ yarrow
- ♦ hibiscus

- lovage
- adam-and-eve root
- strawberry leaves
- black peppercorns
- dragon's blood resin
- damiana
- love oil, rose oil, or love potion

- needle and thread
- Magic Marker
- rose petals
- pink or red candle

Cut open the back of the doll and stuff it with all the ingredients listed above. Sew it up, and with a Magic Marker, write your lover's name over the heart area.

Lay the doll down face up and cover it with rose petals. Light the candle, and let the wax drip over the doll and petals. Take as much time to do this as necessary, sealing all the petals around the doll. Invest each drop of wax with love and your goals for the relationship, always holding the intention that this spell be for the good of all.

On a night of a full moon, bury the poppet in a garden or some special outdoor place to ground your love and to plant it in the earth like a seed that will grow.

Trysting with Power Animals

Witches have familiars; shamans have power animals; many so-called ordinary people have "collectibles": certain animals they have always felt drawn toward and collect as figurines, photos, emblems, or motifs for clothes, greeting cards, and other personal objects. We may have come a long way from our ancestors who lived with animals on a daily basis and even communicated openly with them (in the dreamtime when all living things could speak to each other), but one thing seems to remain fairly constant—animals worm their way into our lives, whether we like it or not! And what power and influence they bestow on us, how they share knowledge, impart their wisdom, teach us the instinctual ways of the earth! People who live a magical life cultivate their animal familiars because they enrich their lives. Lovers could do the same.

If you and your lover already have power animals, you can skip the following step and go on to "Ritual Romp" below. If you do not have power animals, you need to find them or, as shamans like to say, let the animals find you.

CALLING THE ANIMALS

There are various ways to find a power animal. Here are two relatively simple methods. You may already have an animal totem you do not realize is a power animal, one you have always felt drawn toward or collected, or one you always name when asked "What animal would you like to be?" If so, go into alpha, let that animal appear in your mind's eye, and ask it outright if it wants to fulfill the role of animal guide or power animal. Do not feel rejected, if it indicates that it does not want to. This simply means there is another animal who does want to be your power guide, and you should then proceed to explore for it.

One of the most powerful methods to meet a power animal is to journey into the Otherworld, accompanied by the strong, steady beat of a drum or the powerful shaking of a rattle. The sounds of drums and rattles have a unique affinity with animal spirits. These are the sounds of the deep earth. They call forth animal spirits. Even our own blood stirs to their primal music. Forgotten areas of the unconscious open up, ancient memories return, and we instinctually reenter the dreamtime when we knew all things were alive, conscious, and responsive. All things still are, of course. It is we who have forgotten this and have lost the methods of making that communication.

If your lover is willing, you can drum or rattle for each other. If there is no one to accompany you, journey in silence as you would in other deep-consciousness work, using whatever type of trance state comes easily for you. We suggest using the Crystal Countdown as explained earlier.

When you are centered and quiet, move into a landscape containing land, air, and sea: a windy cliffside overlooking the ocean or a breezy shoreline. Go to that place and become aware of these three realms, experiencing each one with as many senses as possible or appropriate, and becoming aware of the profusion of animal life that dwells in them: birds and all the winged ones; fur-bearing animals that run or scamper; fish and sea creatures, and all who swim in the waters of the earth; the horned and hoofed ones who travel in great herds.

Become aware of their presence. Many people doing this journey are startled by a great stampeding, flocking, and swimming of animal spirits. If you experience this, join their dance, either physically or mentally. Become part of the great flow of animal life traversing the earth since earliest times. Celebrate their spirit and power. Eventually you will be drawn to a particular animal, bird, or fish. Move into its presence, or allow it to move into yours, and spend time with it. Talk to it, welcome it, introduce yourself, tell it what you are up to, ask it if it is to be your power animal. The animal will respond in some way. If it indicates no, wait for another, until you encounter your special animal spirit. When you and your power animal have met, and spent some time dancing or hanging out together, thank it, tell it you will be making contact again, and return to ordinary consciousness.

RITUAL ROMP

When you and your lover each have a power animal, you can journey together to the Otherworld and spend time with them. In times of trouble, when your relationship is shaky, it often helps to journey and ask your power animal and your lover's power animal what is wrong and what you can do to make things better. Spirit animals have a certain knowledge and insight we cannot always access on our own. The more we become familiar with them, and they with us, the easier it is to draw on their reservoirs of understanding and wisdom. Sometimes the profoundest insights about our lovers (and ourselves!) are from offhand comments and the shenanigans of power animals.

In happy times, journeying to the Otherworld to run, fly, or swim with power animals is refreshing and empowering as a magical way of spending time with your lover. Shamans believe that what they do "out there" in the Otherworld, even if it is just running with Coyote, or frolicking with Whale, or flying with Raven, has beneficial impact on our ordinary lives. As you strengthen your ties with the animal powers that protect your love relationship, you strengthen the ties of that relationship and deepen your love.

Penny Cabot's Human Candle Spell

Penny offered us this human candle spell to deepen the love between two people. You will need:

♦ two red human candles, one male and one female
♦ one black and one white candle
♦ crushed mandrake root
♦ strawberry leaves
♦ adam-and-eve root (2 pieces)
♦ a deep dish or plate
♦ red string
♦ pieces of rose quartz
♦ rose petals

Light the black and white candles on your altar, the black on the left, the white on the right. Then bore a small hole into the heart area of each human candle (or one hole at each chakra point). Put a small pinch of the love herbs into the hole. Scratch your name on one candle, your lover's on the other.

Face them together on a round plate or deep dish. Write your initials on one piece of adam-and-eve root and your lover's initials on the other. Place the two pieces between the two candles. Then add rose quartz and rose petals on the plate between the candles. Tie the candles with a red string clockwise. Light both candles and let them burn down until the dish is a pool of wax. Let it cool. Remove the wax, now embedded with the other ingredients. Bury it on the night of a full moon for an ongoing relationship or on the night of a new moon for a new relationship.

Lover's Taboos

"I place upon you a *geis* of danger and destruction, O Diarmaid, unless you take me with you out of this house tonight before Finn and the chiefs of Ireland wake from their sleep." With these words Grainne persuaded Diarmaid to elope with her. A *geis* (pronounced "gaysh") is a command, usually expressed as a taboo or prohibition, or in this case, as a task to be performed. Merlin was under a *geis* to return to Vivienne and teach her his magic, even though he knew she would eventually use it against him. The Irish hero Cuchulainn was under a *geis* not to eat the meat of a dog, since the dog was his power animal (his name meant "Dog of Chulain"). The love potion that Iseult gave to Tristan to drink was a type of *geis* that sealed their love for each other, even though it ultimately meant their demise.

A king or hero could be born with certain *geisa* already predicted for his life; others received *geisa* here and there over the course of their lives, often from powerful women, Goddesses, or Faerie lovers. Men, too, such as Druids and wizards, could cast a *geis* on someone. *Geisa* always foretold of danger and misfortune if they were violated. And they almost always were. A series of *geisa* usually enmeshed heroes in a web of prohibitions that were mutually impossible to fulfill. Caught between two conflicting taboos, heroes found themselves in the equivalent of a Celtic Catch-22. When a taboo was violated, it always led to a swift and irrevocable downfall.

Relationships between two lovers frequently have their own versions of the *geis*—certain do's and don'ts that, if violated, will most certainly lead to a turning point in the relationship. Most lovers know what could destroy their relationship, that infraction of trust or commitment which would be, in their partner's eyes, unforgivable and irrevocable. The following spell can be used in two ways: (1) to discover and evaluate the taboos in your relationship, and (2) to strengthen your ability to live up to them.

A *geis* was never cast lightly. There were always serious reasons for it. Every relationship has a spectrum of taboos, some more serious than others. Coming home late, for example, is probably not as serious as having an affair with someone else. Every couple can prioritize the do's and don'ts of their relationship from serious to slight. This ritual journey can be used to learn which are truly the most serious ones.

To begin this spell, we suggest you journey to visit your Inner Partner as explained in Chapter 4. You may, by now, have found other paths to reach or contact your Inner Partner, so use whatever method suits you.

When you are in his/her presence, remain silent for a few moments, collecting your thoughts, allowing the magic of this realm to truly alter your consciousness onto a mystical level. Then, when you feel comfortable, at ease, and ready to learn, state why you have come. Ask, "What is my *geis?* What is it I must not do or risk losing (your lover's name)?"

Let your Inner Partner speak to you in ways appropriate for him or her. Be prepared for a flood of taboos. Unlocking the "taboo vault" is sometimes like opening a chamber filled with crazed bats! A swarm of do's and don'ts, hopes and fears, expectations and apprehensions, may come flocking out. Ask your Inner Partner to help you sort them out, separating the trivial from the truly important ones. Knowing which prohibitions are not really love-threatening is as important as knowing which ones are, so do not be impatient if the dialogue centers primarily on taboos that seem frivolous. This may not be an easy journey to make, for you are in effect asking to know how you can lose your lover. Such knowledge can be difficult, but it is better to know this than to stumble into it unawares.

When you have finished talking over the taboos in your life with your Inner Partner, ask if there is a spell or ritual you could perform to strengthen your ability on a magical level to honor the taboo. Your Inner Partner may give you a spell, or tell you to weave one on your own.

When you are finished, return to ordinary consciousness.

Here are several ways to root your commitment in the physical realm: (1) Find and charge a special stone or charm to carry with you as a reminder of the important obligations to your lover. (2) Tie a knot in a cord for each of the most serious taboos you want to honor. (3) Place springwater outdoors on the night of a full moon and ask the Goddess to enter the water through moonlight and charge it with her strength. Drink some of the water each day, or at times when you feel the need to do so.

Sometimes it is awkward for lovers to discuss taboos with each other openly. But we strongly encourage you to do so at the right time and in the right place. Communication is the key to a strong relationship. It is often easier to bring up touchy subjects if you can present them in the light of your journey to your Inner Partner. You can say to your lover, "My Inner Partner advised me that one of the most important things for our relationship is for me not to ever . . . Do you think that is right? What do you think?" Your lover could suggest a journey to her or his Inner Partner for more information before answering. This type of discussion about intimate issues serves as a buffer to more direct and immediate confrontations. It gives each person time to think, reflect, and seek information from a higher/deeper source. It allows a respite before giving an opinion, and it always presents advice about what the two of you should do as *suggestions* from a third or fourth party, an inner guide. It is like floating trial balloons to see what effect they will have on the other before anything is decided permanently.

Tarot Card Spell

This Tarot card spell from Penny requires an old Tarot deck you no longer need or a new one bought especially for this spell. You can do the spell to strengthen a love relationship or to attract a lover. You will also need:

- a pink or red candle
- rose petals
- a pink cloth
- photos of you and your lover

In a magical space, go through the deck, selecting the love cards. These are any cards that suggest love, romance, desire, commitment, happiness, or any qualities to help strengthen a relationship.

Place rose petals on the first card and drip candle wax on it. While the wax is still wet, lay a second card on top, letting the wax seal them together. Sprinkle rose petals on the second card and drip wax. Then add a third card. Proceed in this manner until all the cards are stacked and sealed with rose petals between them.

Project your love outward into the universe as you stack the cards. If the cards do not stick together, pause and spend some time visualizing your lover and you, renewing your commitment. Then begin again where you left off. If the stack keeps coming apart, then you should really stop and not continue.

When the stack is completely glued together, place a photo of you and your lover, or one of each of you, on top. (If you are doing the spell to attract a lover, put your photo on top and select a Tarot card that best represents the kind of person you are hoping to attract and place it on the bottom.) Wrap the stack and the photos in a pink cloth, and keep the bundle in a bureau drawer or special box. Take it out at night, beginning at a new moon, and expose the cards to moonlight every night until the moon is full or until the spell works. You will know that the spell has worked when your partner shows a renewed interest in you, sex gets better, or whatever specific love intention you did the spell for. If you are looking for a new lover, set the cards in the waxing moonlight each night until he or she appears in your life. When the spell has been accomplished, burn the cards and release the energy.

The Sovereignty Stone

The story of Gawain and Dame Ragnell is possibly one of the most important tales in Western romance literature. And far too few people know it. Here is the gist.

After a series of adventures, Gawain meets at a crossroads a most hideous, foul-smelling woman who claims to know the answer to a question he has been seeking for many months, an answer that, if discovered in time, will prevent the Green Knight from chopping Gawain's head off. (Yes, the story started much earlier. If you're curious, look it up.) The question is: What does a woman want most in all the world? The hag is Dame Ragnell, and she proposes a deal. She will give Gawain the correct answer if he promises to marry her. He agrees, and she tells him that what a woman wants most in all the world is sovereignty. This proves to be the true answer, which saves Gawain's head.

Against advice from other knights that he should drop the old bag, Gawain remains true to his word as an honorable knight of the Round Table and weds the revolting Dame Ragnell. That evening in their bridal chamber, he discovers that she is really a breathtakingly gorgeous woman who has been under an enchantment. But just when Gawain thought he was home safe, Dame Ragnell tells him the hitch (enchantments always seem to come with hitches). The awful news is this: She can only be beautiful twelve out of twenty-four hours each day. She then asks her new husband if he would prefer those twelve hours to be during the day, so that everyone at court could admire her beauty (and Gawain's luck), or at night when they will be alone together in bed.

The legends seem to agree that Gawain did not bang his forehead against the chamber wall or bite his fingernails before replying. He answered immediately. He told Dame Ragnell that she herself should decide which twelve hours she desired to be beautiful. In other words, Gawain gave her sovereignty. And that was the key to breaking the enchantment! From that moment on, Dame Ragnell was always breathtakingly beautiful, twenty-four hours a day.

The following spell concerns personal sovereignty, an ingredient that can make or break a relationship. It is the paradox of freedom within bounds, independence and dependence, being true to oneself while remaining true to the one you love. On some level, in regard to some issues, each of us needs sovereignty, and sensitive lovers respect that need in their partners and allow them to exercise it. Most often sovereignty is denied because one lover wants to change something "ugly" in the other. We want our lovers to be perfect twenty-four hours a day. No one can be perfect twenty-four hours a day. Twelve hours max! And even that is asking a lot! At some point lovers must allow their mates to be themselves. (This is not the same issue as tolerating a partner's "rough edges" when those rough edges are truly dangerous. An alcoholic or physically abusive partner should not be given sovereignty to pursue behavior that puts you in jeopardy. Each person must use good judgment in drawing the line regarding acceptable and unacceptable behavior.)

Go on a quest for a "sovereignty stone" in a creek bed or forest or along a shoreline. Select one that you can carry easily in a pocket or bag if you want to make it a charm to keep with you. A larger stone is fine if you plan to leave it in some special place. The sovereignty stone should be, like Dame Ragnell under the wicked enchantment, half beautiful and half ugly. Your own aesthetic sense will decide this. It might be smooth on one side, and rough on the other; clear on one side, speckled on the other; whole on one side, cracked or gouged on the other; or the sides might be of different colors or shades.

Honor this stone in some special way. Bless it when you return home with air, fire, water, and earth. Grant it the right to be just the way it is, half beautiful and half ugly. The Goddess tumbled this stone for centuries making it just what it is today, and there is nothing wrong with it. It is perfect, in her sight, and state firmly that it is also perfect in your sight. See the stone as whole, just as you are trying to see your lover as whole. Grant the stone sovereignty. Say, "Stone of the Earth, I give you the right to be just what you are." The more you try to say this and sound sincere, the sillier you will sound, because you know that the stone is going to be what it is with or without your permission!

Now let the stone represent your lover, and assign what you

perceive as his or her "negative" qualities to the ugly side; and spend an equal amount of time, of course, attributing your lover's positive qualities to the beautiful side. Then picture the stone as your lover, and say, "You are the Love of my life; I give you the right to be just what you are." This time you should not sound silly. However, you may not sound absolutely sincere! If not, work on it. The stone will help you. Keep the stone, turning it over every twelve hours, morning and night, to allow it to be both beautiful and ugly. Or carry it in your pocket, and pull it out every now and then to see whether its gorgeous or hideous side first meets your eye. Seek the stone's help to become absolutely sincere. (Sincerity does not mean you have to *like* your lover's flaws; sincerity means you allow your lover to have them.)

You'll know the spell has worked when one of two things happens: (1) You no longer criticize your lover for his/her flaws, and (2) you check out the stone one day, and it is so beautiful on both sides that you can barely stand to look at it!

Dragon's Blood Love Spell

Here is a spell to increase love between you and your loved one. You will need:

- 6-inch square of red cotton cloth
- a teaspoon of dragon's blood powder
- three straight pins
- one red and one black candle
- 6-inch square of parchment paper
- one metal plate, ash pot, or metal bowl
- love potion

In a sacred space hold the candles and visualize you and your lover, and ask the Goddess and God that this spell be for the good of all and that it work quickly. Anoint the candles with love potion. Then place the black candle to the left, the red to the right, with the ash pot between them.

Cut a heart shape out of the red fabric and another out of the parchment. Write on the parchment heart:

> *Heart of Love, spell me this spell.*
> *The one I do love will love me as well.*
> *So mote it be.*

Put a few drops of love potion on both hearts. Stick the pins into the cloth heart, concentrating on your love. Repeat the spell out loud on each pin. Leave the pins in the heart. Then place the cloth and parchment hearts in the ash pot and sprinkle the dragon's blood on them. Then light them. As the hearts burn, hold your hands over the heat and watch the smoke rise. Visualize the two of you together and say out loud, "So mote it be."

When the flame goes out, take the remains (ashes, pieces of paper or cloth, the pins) and place them on a plate. Melt the red candle wax over them. When it cools, put the wax in a magic bag and carry it with you, or place it somewhere in your bedroom.

The Oak and Holly Lovers

Gay men and lesbians often experience a unique tension in their relationships because the opposites and polarities in their love for each other can be obscured by the similarities of being the same sex. But opposites attract in gay relationships, as they do in straight relationships. And the similarities, as gay and lesbian couples know, can be a source of strength and stability, since they provide a basis for a deep understanding of one's partner that couples of different sexes never experience.

Here is a spell for gay male lovers based on the ritual combat of the Oak King and Holly King as they reign over different halves of the year.

The Oak King represents the half of the year from December 21 to June 21, a time when the sun is waxing, days are growing longer and warmer, the earth is preparing to burst forth in new life. His totem is the robin, a bird traditionally associated with the return of spring and the emergence of new life. The Holly King assumes ascendance from June 21 to December 21, a season when the sun's power wanes, days grow shorter, the weather turns colder, the harvest is maturing, the earth prepares for its winter respite. His totem is the wren, a bird associated with eaves and chimneys, a house-bird that nests in the snug safety of the hearth.

In folklore the two kings engage in ritual combat at the turning points of the year, the old king being slain to make room for the younger king. Neither is actually killed, of course, but withdraws when his six-month reign is up. The kings are twins of sorts, each being the other's alternate side. In the yearly struggles of the Oak and Holly Kings we see replayed the tension of opposites, even though within each is the other, and without the other, each would be only half of a never completed whole. Both are necessary.

Gay men can draw on this myth to appreciate differences between them, reconcile opposite characteristics, and learn to defer to each other's strengths and support the other in his time of weakness.

Since the human mind is quick to see polarities, it should not be hard for two gay lovers to determine which of them is the Oak King and which the Holly King. In broad terms, we are looking for "oak" and "waxing" qualities: stronger, physically larger, more extroverted, expansive, outgoing, brighter, effusive, cocky, growing. The other contains the "holly" and "waning" qualities: gentler, smaller, more introverted, retiring, darker, reserved, diminishing.

Since everything contains its opposite, both oak and holly traits can be found in every person to some degree. Also, different times and circumstances bring out certain qualities and discourage others, so one man will probably not exhibit oak or holly traits consistently and exclusively. And one other point, these polarities are not moral terms. Dark and gentle, for example, are not "bad" compared to bright and tough. Everything on the great Wheel of Life has a place and purpose.

Gay lovers can acknowledge the healthy rivalry of opposite character traits by constructing an oak and holly shrine on an altar with leaves and branches from the two trees, or by placing an oak and holly arrangement in a bedroom or some other room. Collect the items for the shrine together on a special hike, and spend some time during this day discussing the different ways Oak and Holly Kings as archetypes manifest in each of you. The more that lovers can openly and honestly look at and appreciate their differences, find value in them, and create a nonthreatening context in which to discuss them, the easier it is to accept each other when times are rocky or when arguments erupt.

Charge, bless, and arrange the items in a ritual similar to the one explained in the "Lovers' Branch Ritual" on pages 194–95.

Recite the following spells to each other.

The "holly partner" says:

> *King of the Acorn, King of the Oak,*
> *Growing strong in crown and cloak*
> *Of bud and leaf and waxing sun,*
> *I follow the course in which you run.*
> *I tread your path, O King of the Oak,*
> *Leading to flowers and summer smoke.*

The "oak partner" can honor his mate with:

> *King of the Holly, lead the way*
> *From hearty crops to harvest day,*
> *I follow the path on which you run*
> *A path ever green through the waning sun.*
> *When winter blows the leaves away,*
> *O Holly King, my love will stay.*

Memorize these verses and call them to mind when you need to renew your appreciation for the differences between you.

The Demeter–Kore Lovers

Lesbian couples can draw inspiration from the Greek legend of Demeter and Kore, building on the mother–daughter dynamic to discover the different ways each woman is sometimes the nurturer and at other times the one who needs nurturing.

The heart of the Demeter–Kore legend is the abduction of the young Kore one day while pursuing a narcissus flower in a field. The earth opened up, and Hades grabbed the young woman and took her to his underworld realm. Heartbroken over her loss, Demeter searched for her daughter, refusing to allow the earth to provide crops for food. Eventually Zeus sent Hermes to the Underworld to persuade Hades to allow Kore to return. Hades agreed, but made her eat some pomegranate seeds first, the symbol of their indissoluble marriage. So for a part of each year Kore returns to Hades, where she reigns as Persephone, Queen of the Underworld.

Since appreciation of differences is a key to any relationship, it is incumbent upon same-sex couples to recognize those differences and accept them as healthy diversity. Too easily can these differences be ignored or obscured by the similarities inherent in lesbian or gay relationships. Looking for broad trends, each woman should be able to assign "mother" or "daughter" qualities to herself and her partner. It may be that one is more consistently "mother" or "daughter" than the other, or it might be that the mother–daughter traits are fairly evenly distributed between the two women. Also, keep in mind that different situations will draw out "mother" or "daughter" qualities in both partners, so we are not expecting one partner to be a complete Demeter to the other's complete Kore.

Demeter traits might include: being more dependent, domestic, possessive, exclusive, nurturing, being older, wiser, more experienced, educated, and physically larger. Kore qualities can include: being more independent, sociable, outgoing, needing more nurturing, being younger and wilder, less experienced, less educated, and physically smaller.

Place a Demeter–Kore picture or sculpture on an altar or in a bedroom as a commitment to honor and respect the differences in each other. View the tension that arises in your relationship in terms of "mother–daughter" traits. Let the mother–daughter paradigm provide a nonthreatening vocabulary for discussing ways to reconcile differences.

A ritual similar to the Lovers' Branch Ritual, on pages 194–

95 or the gay men's ritual on pages 226–27 can be performed using wheat, corn, or other grain for Demeter, and pomegranates or narcissus for Kore.

Each woman can honor the other by reciting these verses: The "Kore woman" can say:

> *Mother of Earth, where love is born,*
> *Strong in soil, root, and thorn,*
> *Protect the home and find the child*
> *Through wandering paths that cross the wild.*
> *Mother of Earth, of wheat and corn,*
> *Your circle of love turns night to morn.*

The "Demeter partner" can say:

> *Daughter of Earth, may I learn*
> *To love the ways of petal and fern,*
> *The flowers that lure you over the field,*
> *The gifts in which your heart is sealed.*
> *Daughter of Earth, my heart will burn*
> *For you, for us, for spring's return.*

Each woman can use these lines as reminders of the importance that diversity plays in a relationship, and to recognize the many ways that a loving couple can care for each other, in giving and receiving love.

British Celtic Love Spell

Here is Jody's favorite spell to do when you and your lover are separated. It is intended for obtaining safe return and happy reunion. You will need:

- ◆ 2 cups springwater
- ◆ 2 tablespoons sea salt
- ◆ 2 hairs of a white cow
- ◆ 2 hairs of a white bull (In modern times we must make some substitutions! Live, shedding cats and dogs will do. Take two hairs from the male and two from the female.)
- ◆ 3 clover leaves
- ◆ 3 roses
- ◆ 2 willow leaves

Bring the water to a boil in a cauldron or metal pot. Add the sea salt, stir, then add all the other ingredients. Reduce heat to simmer, and say:

> *By my birth of the two serpents,*
> *I call the Goddess Cerridwen*
> *and the God Celi to send me*
> *on their magical moonship*
> *to my lover's side.*
> *The wren sets the cauldron to boil*
> *and brings life to the sacred land.*
> *Bring me to my lover's side*
> *and let us love hand in hand.*

Use the brew as a love potion or allow it to simmer on your stove.

Ring of Hearts Spell

Here is a lovers' spell for two people. It should be done in a
playful manner so it brings out the child in each of you as you
sit on the floor and cut out paper hearts. You will need:

- ◆ red paper, a black pen, a scissors
- ◆ red thread and a needle
- ◆ a small round mirror
- ◆ one red candle and one brown candle

Cut twelve red hearts and place them in a ring. Write your
lover's name on six of the hearts, as he or she writes your name
on the other six. Lay the mirror down flat, and place the hearts
around it, alternating yours and your partner's. Light the candles. Red is for passion and love, and to rejuvenate sex and
sensual feelings for each other. Brown will bring love to the
environment where you perform the spell. (If this is in your
home, it will increase the love atmosphere there. If it is outside,
it will create a good love field others will pick up on when they
pass through it.)

Bend over and look down into the mirror, and repeat your
lover's name six times, each time picking up a heart with his or
her name. Then your partner does this. Next, sew one of your
hearts to one of your lover's. Then he or she adds one with your
name. Continue until they are all sewn together in one packet.
Hang the packet of hearts in an appropriate room or some
erotic place, such as near the fireplace, the bed, the sauna.

Handfasting

Here is a favorite way that my coven handfasts a couple. The marriage can be sealed for a lifetime or for a year and a day, at which time the couple may renew their union or let it dissolve.

Cast a nine-foot-diameter circle and strew nosegays, flowers, and ribbons around the circumference. The immediate family and other Witches and close friends stand just inside the circle to form an inner ring around the altar draped in pink, white, and black cloth. Frankincense and myrrh or other love incenses are kept burning during the entire ritual. Two chalices filled with wine or springwater stand between one white and one black candle. Next to the chalices are two wedding rings.

The bride and groom are led into the circle from the north. Once inside, the high priestess casts the circle with her wand, and the bride and groom greet the powers of the four directions as they walk around the circle. Next the priestess sweeps the circle with a Witch's broom, brushing away all harmful events in the couple's past lives. The lovers kneel facing each other; the priestess charges the rings and chalices. Next the couple casts their verbal spell to seal their commitment to each other while looking into each other's eyes. The spell states in their own words their love for each other and the goals the two share for this union.

Each lover picks up the other's wedding ring and drops it into the opposite chalice. Then each picks up the chalice containing his or her ring, and they cross forearms so the priestess can bind them loosely with the black silk cord draped in a figure eight. Next they take a sip from the other's chalice. The rest is poured into a bowl, the rings removed and placed on the hands of the bride and groom. The priestess then removes the silk cord, holds it over the heads of the couple, and pulls the loosely bound knot tight as she says, "I tie the knot." Next she gives one end of the cord to each lover for them to hold between them as a symbol of their handfasting. The high priestess places a hand on each one's head and announces to them and the witnesses, "You are bound in the sight of the Goddess and God as husband and wife. So mote it be."

Then the priestess charges all the wedding gifts and magical presents placed under the altar before the ritual began. The circle is opened. The merriment begins!

Spells to End Relationships

IN SOME LEGENDS of deceased lovers, a tree grows from each one's grave, leaning toward the other as if some irrepressible magic draws them together in death until finally their branches lovingly intertwine. So, too, are we sometimes inclined toward a wayward lover, hoping our separate lives might once again wrap around each other. Breaking up is as hard to do as grieving for a deceased loved one. When a relationship ends for whatever reason—incompatibility, unfaithfulness, boredom—our hearts can go through an emotional whirlwind: anger, grief, guilt, resentment, despondence. At this time magic can help. Here are some spells to lighten the circumstances surrounding the end, the beginning of the end, and the aftermath of love.

Spell for a Smooth Breakup

Jody recommends to do this spell before you part, projecting a friendly split, wishing your partner well. Remember that what you cast with magic returns to you threefold. You will need:

♦ two red paper hearts
♦ two 2-foot lengths of red cord or string
♦ hole punch
♦ love potion
♦ a black pen
♦ rose petals
♦ two pink candles, two white candles
♦ frankincense and myrrh

Anoint the four candles and light them. Burn the incense to purify the space and to neutralize the love between you and the lover you are leaving.

Write your name on one heart, your lover's on the other, and lay each one on your altar between a pink and a white candle. Sprinkle rose petals on the hearts. Pick up the heart with your name and say: "This heart is mine. I will find love. I will love myself and have comfort in my life without the loving company of (name your partner)." Lay the heart back down

Pick up the other heart and repeat the spell saying: "This heart is (lover's name). He/she will find love, etc."

Hold the hearts together and punch a hole in them and insert both strings through holes. Lay the hearts back down on the altar. Look at them and begin to envision your separation from your lover. See it as a peaceful, calm transition. While contemplating this, pull your lover's heart and string from your heart. Do this slowly and gently, as you project an amicable separation. The hearts are now apart with a string through each. Tie the ends of each string together to form a loop for hanging.

After you leave the circle, hang your heart where you can see it. Hang your soon-to-be-ex's heart somewhere where you will not see it, perhaps deep in the woods on a tree. Or put it in an envelope, write a phony name and address on it, and mail it to a distant town where it will end up in the dead-letter office.

Spell to Let Go of a Lover

This spell comes from Kate Armant, a Witch who lives in the Berkshire Mountains of western Massachusetts.

Take a photograph of you and your ex-lover depicting a time or event in the past when the relationship was still good for both of you. Then cut out the ex-lover's image.

Cast a circle and burn the image while envisioning a hopeful, joyful life without this person. Do not blame yourself or your ex-lover, nor hold any thoughts of recrimination or revenge while engaged in this meditation. Continue the projection of your future life for a few minutes.

Bury the ashes in an appropriate place.

Telephone Spell

My daughter Penny recommends this spell to encourage an estranged lover to call when you need to talk. If you call your ex first, or too many times, it will look as if you are still chasing him or her. But sometimes you really do need to talk, so here is a spell to get your ex-lover to call you. You will need:

- ♦ an orange magic bag
- ♦ an orange candle, a black candle, a white candle
- ♦ herbs: parsley, mandrake, flaxseed, celery, cloves, holly-hock, thyme
- ♦ a glass bowl
- ♦ love potion
- ♦ a 12-inch red ribbon

Anoint all three candles and place the black on the left, the white on the right; then light them. Hold the orange candle in your hands, and envision your ex-lover picking up the phone and dialing your number. Place the orange candle between the other two and light it.

Mix the herbs and add a few drops of love oil. Hold your hands over the bowl and say:

> Bring to me my heart's desire:
> Telephone ring!
> Have his/her love come through the wire:
> Telephone ring!

Again see your ex-lover's face, see him/her making the call and talking sweetly to you.

Place the herbs in the orange bag, and tie it to the telephone cord with the red ribbon. Set a limit for the spell, such as several days or a week. If your ex has not called by then, repeat the spell.

Spell for Protection Against an Abusive Lover

By invoking the help of an appropriate God or Goddess as explained in Chapter 6, we can sometimes soften a lover's bad temper, inconsiderateness, or bitchiness. But there are times when a truly abusive and dangerous partner cannot be handled this way. His or her baneful energy is too strong. Here is a protection spell for this kind of situation. You will need:

♦ one white candle, one black candle
♦ two silver pentacles
♦ one rose quartz, preferably set in jewelry
♦ 2 tablespoons dittany of Crete
♦ 2 tablespoons eyebright
♦ a pinch of wolf's hair
♦ one black and one white feather
♦ two 2-foot lengths of cord or string
♦ protection potion
♦ black moon potion
♦ parchment paper and black ink pen
♦ ash pot
♦ frankincense and myrrh
♦ earthen bowl

At the dark of the moon or during a waning moon, cast a circle. Anoint the candles with protection potion and black moon potion, and place the black candle on the left and the white candle on the right. While anointing the black candle say, "Give me power to neutralize any harm coming my way from anyone or anything. So mote it be." While anointing the white candle, say, "I send your light to bind and neutralize anyone or anything that may bring me harm. So mote it be."

Burn frankincense and myrrh between the candles, saying, "I neutralize and make pure this sacred circle."

Place the quartz, pentacles, dittany of Crete, wolf hair, and eyebright in the bowl and add a few drops of both potions.

Write on the parchment paper:

> *"My love does often bind*
> *and does not keep clear of my mind,*
> *to stop the pain, to break the chain*
> *I neutralize those near*
> *and keep love that's dear."*

With your fingertip put a drop of both potions on the paper and recite the spell out loud, holding the paper over the smoke. Then burn the parchment in the white candle's flame and drop the burning paper into the ash pot. When the fire goes out, put the ashes in the earthen bowl so they touch the quartz and the two pentacles.

Hold the black feather in your left hand and pass it through the incense smoke, saying, "Safety in love, fly to me. Spirit of Feather, protect me."

Do the same with the white feather in your right hand, saying, "Send the message loud and strong that my love knows no bounds except those of abusive anger. Spirit of Feather, keep all harm from me. So mote it be."

Pass your hands over the bowl, saying, "These enchanted things shall protect my loving nature from all harm. So mote it be."

You now have several talismans of protection to place in your home, car, or on your person. Wear the quartz jewelry or put it in a pink bag and tie it to your clothing. Put one pentacle on the black cord, and wear it. Place the other pentacle somewhere in your home. Keep the feathers on or near you, perhaps in your car. Keep the herbs and ashes in the bowl somewhere nearby.

As we advised in Chapter 1, what you do in a magical realm should be complemented by parallel action in the physical realm. In addition to a protection spell, seek outside help to safeguard yourself against physical harm.

Spell to Become Invisible

Sometimes after a couple breaks up, they continue to run into each other at local places or in the company of mutual friends. In Scotland the Faeries placed a "glamoric" on people and objects to change their shape or make them invisible. Here is a spell to make yourself invisible so that your ex-lover either won't see you or won't see in you the problems that broke up your relationship. You will need:

- three candles: green, black, white
- dried fiddlefern
- heather
- one appleseed
- two willow leaves
- one oak leaf
- parchment and pen with green ink
- a green talisman such as necklace, button, socks, hat
- wear plaid fabric (your own tartan if you have it)

Cast a circle. Light the candles and mix the herbs, seed, and leaves to make an incense mixture. Burn it, and let the smoke rise around you.

On the parchment write the following three times:

Queen Mab, fith-fath, fath-fith.

Mab is a Faerie Queen and "fith-fath fath-fith" a fairy charm. Recite what you have written three times out loud over the talisman, holding it close to your lips. Then hold the talisman and the parchment over the smoke, letting the scent envelop and penetrate both. Wear the talisman and keep the parchment with you when you want to be invisible.

Cleansing Love Bath

This bath with special herbs will ease melancholy and bring a sense of peace and tenderness. You will need:

- 1 ounce dried roses
- ½ ounce comfrey root
- 1 ounce of each: red clover, nettle, red hibiscus, sea salt
- ten drops love potion
- a large bowl
- a large facecloth
- 2-foot ribbon of lavender, pink, or red

Cast a circle. Mix all the ingredients in a bowl and charge the mixture to purify your heart, mind, and spirit, freeing them from all injurious energies. Ask the Goddess Mab to cleanse your body and aura from everything in your past love that still lingers and hurts, and to infuse you with self-esteem and new love that will continue strong after the bath.

On a Friday or a day and hour of Venus, draw a hot bath. Place the herbal mixture in the facecloth, and tie it with the ribbon, making a pouch. Put the bundle into the bath, like a tea bag. Anoint with love potion, and light as many pink, green, lavender, or red candles as you wish. Use the bath for a long one-hour soak. Do not wash with soap or shampoo. If you need to wash, take a shower before the bath. When the bath is over, get out and pat yourself dry with a towel.

Spell to Neutralize the Influence of a Third Party

Sometimes we sense a change of habits or a different look in our lover's eyes and we know intuitively that a third party has intruded into our relationship. Suspicions rise. Our partner or spouse has either been unfaithful or is being tempted. Here is a spell from Andrew Jackson, a Salem Witch, to discern the identity of the "other man or woman" and to build up self-esteem while neutralizing the intruder's power to destroy your relationship. There are three parts to this spell.

Part One: During a waxing moon, wear a gold ring with a bloodstone on the sun finger of your left hand to give you courage and knowledge about the intruding person. On a Wednesday at 1:00 P.M. or 8:00 P.M., anoint a large candle with wintergreen oil, and call upon all the influences of Mercury to give you the knowledge you need, such as the name, sex, appearance, and age of the third party. Scribe this spell:

"I call upon a celestial body, the planet nearest the Sun, Mercury with all your knowledge and wisdom. A person I seek. To me must come a name, an age, a place of home. For my well-being is why I ask. To thee O God and Goddess, I do task to grant me this knowledge clear and free by new moon next for harmony."

Look for the information by the next new moon.

Part Two: Andy calls this visualization SEVER: Self-Esteem Visualization Enforcing Relationships. Do it during a waxing moon and at an hour of Venus. Light a pink candle anointed with wormwood oil. Put on some of your spouse's perfume or cologne to enhance his or her presence.

Relax and shift consciousness so that you see the two of you during the good times, free of pressures and totally committed to each other. Experience loving feelings from the past and project them to your mate so he or she will pick up these old memories and continue to value them and the love you had for each other earlier in your relationship.

Place hibiscus flowers on your altar or carry them in a green or pink bag on your right side to keep your name and image strong in your lover's dreams.

Repeat this visualization three times on different days and hours of Venus to secure the spell.

Part Three: At a waning moon make a Black Tower Binding Philter with the following:

- ♦ five parts Virginia snake root
- ♦ three parts black malva flowers
- ♦ three parts galanga
- ♦ 1 dram melissa oil (garden balm)

Recite the following incantation while you mix the ingredients:

> *Sacred herbs, sacred herbs,*
> *On this day and magical hour*
> *I call upon your wondrous power.*
> *It's a cleansing of energy that I need*
> *Take this intruder behind my leave,*
> *And with your best protective power*

Guide the invader's love to the tower
To keep this love safe from me
Keep the lock and toss the key.
Thank you for this wondrous chance
To cleanse my favorite romance.
Now if it's meant to be
Return my lover back to me.
With free will for the good of all
So mote it be.

Then repeat the SEVER visualization but with the following addition: See you and your lover earlier in your relationship when your love was strong and fresh, as you did in Part Two. But now incorporate a vision of the third party watching the two of you enjoying each other's company and love. Let your love for each other build up as a wall around you and see the adversary watching your love and trust shut him or her out. Project this tower of love to the intruder so that he or she realizes it will be difficult to scale the walls. If your love is still correct, the third party will not be able to invade your tower of safety. If it is indeed time for your relationship to end, the competitor will easily scale the walls.

Bottle Spell to Neutralize Harmful Influences

This spell is meant to bind an abusive lover's power to harm you physically or to spread gossip about you. This is the spell we offer to those in pain and danger. It is not a hex on the other nor a spell to do harm. As Witches we take the Code of the Craft seriously to do spells only for the good of all; and we believe the results of every spell return threefold to the one who casts it. In this respect, a binding spell is no threat to the magic-worker because we should want our own power to do harm to be equally bound.

Our advice to readers being harassed by a hateful ex-lover is just the opposite of baneful magic. We suggest love magic for the ex-lover, in addition to the protection spell for yourself. Select an appropriate spell from Chapter 5, and cast it so your ex-partner will fall in love with someone new, be happy, and have no time to make life miserable for you.

For this spell you will need:

♦ 4 tablespoons frankincense or myrrh
♦ 4 tablespoons black powdered iron
♦ 4 tablespoons sea salt
♦ 4 tablespoons orris-root powder or oak moss
♦ one white candle
♦ one bottle with a cork or lid
♦ parchment paper and black ink pen
♦ black thread

Mix the sea salt, orris-root powder, and iron in a bowl. Cut a piece of parchment that will fit inside the bottle and write on it with black ink, "I neutralize the power of (name adversary) to do me any harm. I ask that this be correct and for the good of all. So mote it be."

Roll up the parchment, tie it with a black thread to bind it, and place it in the bottle. Fill the bottle with the dry ingredients. Then take the white candle and, while turning the bottle counterclockwise, drip wax over the cork to seal it. Last, secretly bury the bottle in a place where it will not be disturbed, and no animal or person will dig it up. This spell is like a genie trapped in a bottle. It should never be unleashed or the power of the spell is lost.

Spell to Release Anger

Let's face it: you're angry! When anger, a form of energy, is directed to worthwhile purposes, it can be beneficial, but often estranged lovers harbor anger beyond its usefulness. It hinders them from getting on with their lives. Here is a spell to release anger and send it back into the universe where it becomes neutral energy. You will need:

- a glass item, if possible a wineglass, plate, or other glass object your lover used to use, but any glass bottle or jar will do
- some black paint

Paint your lover's name or initials on the glass. Take it to the local dump or recycling center. Go into alpha and transfer your anger into the glass object. Spend as much time doing this as you need until you feel you have released all your anger, or as much as possible. Then summon all your strength, close your eyes, and throw the glass as hard as you can into the dump. Listen to it shatter. Smile. Then walk away and don't look back.

Eulogy Spell for a Deceased Lover

This eulogy can be said at a funeral or at the graveside of a deceased lover. It can be part of a more elaborate ritual in which you remove a small amount of topsoil from the grave for your altar, or plant a crystal in the soil, or insert your athame into the grave soil to let the energy from your lover's body charge the metal.

"Like a rock descending a mountainside, death has come. No one knew the heart of flesh in his/her breast save the wail of my heart, the sobbing of my soul for him/her. How I long to be beside you in life once again. Alone I wish you a safe journey into the enchanted land. The God and Goddess come to the center of the crystal bridge beckoning you to cross to the land of apples and songbirds. Turn and wave farewell to me if you can. Watch me from your Island of Hearts. I love you always."

Old Formula to Express Grief

When the Faerie Cael died, his beloved Credhe lamented, "Why should I not die of grief for my mate? Even restless wild creatures die of sorrow after him." Then she spoke this simple but powerful statement of grief:

> *The thrush of Drum Queen admits a woeful note.*
> *In Letterlee the blackbird makes his wail.*
> *In Drumlish the deer makes sad moan*
> *And the stag laments his doe has died.*
> *Sore suffering to me is the death of the hero,*
> *The death of him who used to lie by my side.*
> *Now he lies dead beside me swept by the waves,*
> *He who was so delightful to me.*

Nature's Magical Tools

WE LIVE IN a magical world bursting with energy. Nature is a great reservoir of limitless wisdom and power, with myriad material things, each containing an inner spirit that is alive, conscious, and responsive to people whose perceptions delve beneath its physical shape. The goal of magic is change and transformation, and it uses the energies within natural objects and familiar symbols.

Folk magic—the magical practices of average men and women—have always drawn on the commonplace objects of the natural world and standard household utensils. Elaborate devices, expensive equipment, and complex systems of arcane philosophy have seldom appealed to the common person, nor been readily available. Indeed, folk wisdom clearly shows they are not necessary. Each of us is surrounded with natural tools of power and energy, and we have listed the major ones here for you to use in the spells and rituals presented in this book and in magical practices you create yourself.

Over the centuries individual flowers, herbs, stones, patterns, colors, and animals have acquired reputations for certain powers, and modern magic-workers are wise in following the experience of the past. But we should also trust our instincts and the secret voice of nature speaking to us directly to explore, innovate, and experiment. We can rediscover or discover for the first time how to apply the objects of the natural world to empower our magic.

Science claims that every physical object in the universe exerts an attraction of some degree on every other object. The entire cosmos thus holds itself together in a divine embrace. Is this not the very law of love that mystics of every culture have experienced? These same elements and patterns of energy attracting each other across the great web of the cosmos can shape our own spells to create, renew, or strengthen that attraction between two people we call love.

We are part of nature and share a common language with our brothers and sisters in the animal, vegetable, and mineral realms. If we no longer hear or understand this language, it is due not to nature's silence but to our dulled powers of perception. With practice, attunement, and a humble respect for forces greater than ourselves, we will hear the voice of the natural world once again inviting us to reclaim our cosmic heritage, our birthright as children of the Great Mother. All acts of love and pleasure are hers, even as these same acts of pleasure and love are her gifts to us. The simple lists below contain the links between her great love for us and our love for one another.

STONES

Stones are ancient. Whether giant boulders that rib the mountains or the smooth pebbles tumbled by the ocean, each stone contains worlds of whirling energy beneath its hard, mute surface. A renewed interest in the spiritual power of stones has made many people familiar with the properties of various stones and gems. Here are some especially appropriate for love spells.

Love Stones

- pink quartz
- clear quartz
- rhodochrosite
- sugilite,
- pearl
- water pearl
- malachite
- emerald
- pink tourmaline
- green tourmaline
- watermelon tourmaline
- pink coral
- diamond

Birthstones

Often I combine a birthstone with a love stone when doing a spell for a particular person. The two stones together increase the magic.

- January: kunzite, jasper, geodes, fluorite, calcite, amazonite
- February: amethyst, alexandrite, alexandrine, mica
- March: jasper, aqua-aura, bloodstone, quarmarine, blue topaz, herkimer diamond
- April: diamond, ruby, garnet, pyrite, hematite, lava
- May: emerald, beryl, moss agate, malachite, pink calcite
- June: pearl, moonstone, rhodochrosite, rose quartz, watermelon tourmaline, marble
- July: peridot, yellow citrine, cat's-eye, aventurine, sunstones, yellow diamond
- August: carnelian, opal, amber, yellow topaz
- September: agate, sugilite, smoky quartz
- October: obsidian, red or black coral, ruby, petrified wood
- November: turquoise, lapis lazuli, amethyst
- December: black onyx, hematite, ruby, sugilite

HERBS/FRUIT

When picking herbs or fruit for spells, trust your inner feelings about which ones to use. Cast a circle around the plant first, ask its permission to take it or part of it, express your thanks if it consents, and try to leave part of the plant or companion plants so the area is not depleted. If possible, break off stems and leaves with your fingers, or cut with a ritual knife rather than a scissors. Here are some lists of plants that are powerful for love spells.

Herbs/Fruit

- Apple
- Aster
- Caraway
- Coriander
- Cumin
- Jasmine
- Lavender
- Lovage
- Marjoram
- Meadowsweet
- Myrtle
- Nettle
- Orange
- Orris
- Rosemary
- Tormentil
- Vervain
- Violet
- Yarrow

FLOWERS

The beauty, fragrance, and delicacy of flowers make them obvious metaphors for so much that we want to say about love. Not only magical spells but social customs have yoked flowers and love. Here are the love values for flowers you may want to use in spells or to send to your lover.

- Amaryllis (belladone): You are beauty.
- Anemone: I cast you away.
- Bluebell: I bind with Faerie magic.
- Camellia: Beauty beyond this world.
- Carnation: To mend a broken heart.
- Chrysanthemum: To draw in the magic of love.
- Clematis: Beauty of the Otherworld and sexual attraction.
- Columbine: A fool's heart cannot be broken.
- Cornflower: To draw love and sex.
- Daffodil: Power of the Faerie Queen; to find love.
- Daisy: Lasting love; to love through the Wheel of the Year.
- Dandelion: Psychic message of love.
- Forget-me-not: To remind a lover of you.
- Foxglove: To learn about a false lover.
- Gentian: To find a secret lover.
- Hollyhock: I shall achieve my goals in love.
- Honeysuckle: Sweet taste of love.
- Hyacinth: To purge your heart of love.
- Iris: I bind my love.
- Ivy: To bind love and honor.
- Jasmine: To bring abundance of love.
- Lavender: To learn the secrets of love.
- Lilac: To tell if love is real or not.

- Lily: To cleanse one's heart of pain.
- Marigold: I must leave you.
- Narcissus: I love myself more than you.
- Nasturtium: I trust my love.
- Orchid: Night love and mystery.
- Pansy: Dreams of love.
- Peony: I draw love unabashedly.
- Phlox: To show love for another.
- Poppy: To send moon Faeries to whisper your name.
- Primrose: To appear youthful and loving.
- Rose: Love, the Goddess.
- Speedwell: To send love fast and far.
- Sunflower: To win love.
- Tulip: To claim your lover.
- Violet: To balance the mind of a lover.
- Wisteria: To shower love everywhere.
- Water lily: To send water Faeries with messages of love.

The Rose

Many of the spells in the preceding chapters suggest the use of roses or rose petals because the flower has long been a symbol of love and consequently is sacred to the Goddess. Here are some of the many secrets and meanings roses have for Witches. If you have access to a variety of roses, select the one that best expresses your intentions for a given spell.

- Austrian Rose: To bring the look of beauty to each of us
- Bridal Rose: To bind a marriage spell to last for eternity

- Bud of a Moss Rose: To bring the light from the planet Venus to charge a written spell
- Bud of a Red Rose: To wear in a wedding and to bring passion into your life
- Bud of a White Rose: To bring the Faerie Queen's blessing on your love relationship
- Bud with thorns and leaves: To keep a wrong and unwanted lover away
- Bud stripped of thorns: To make the way easy for new lovers to declare themselves
- Burgundy Rose: To bind dreams of you in your lover's mind
- Cabbage Rose: To remind your lover of you by projecting the scent of rose
- Pink Rose: To begin a love affair and to increase self-love
- Provence Rose: To charm a lover into seeing your face in his or her dreams
- Red, White, and Pink Roses together: To promote fertility
- Red Rose: The Goddesses Cerridwen, Macha, and Morgain will bless you with love.
- Rose leaf: To mend your broken heart
- Single Rose: To bring a new lover into your life
- Thornless Rose: To rid a love affair of arguments and trouble
- Tudor Rose: To bring sovereignty and peace in the home
- White Rose: To grant the love of Oonah, the Faerie Queen
- Withered Red Rose: To rid your mind of an unfaithful lover
- Withered White Rose: To release the painful memories of a love passed away

♦ Yellow Rose: To tell if a lover is untrue, or to tell who is
gossiping about you

In addition to being a statement of love, the rose has also
been valued for its contribution to folk medicines. In the eigh-
teenth century a third of all European herbal remedies utilized
some part of the rose. The rose has had special meaning and
importance since pagan times as a flower of love, healing, passion, and even death. At one time the Christian church tried to
ban its use as a funeral flower but eventually gave up in the face
of widespread opposition on the part of common folk who
continued to use the flower as an expression of love and life
even in the rites of death.

SEEDS, ROOTS, BULBS, LEAVES

For magical objects or powders for potions we use parts of the
plant. Here is a list of plants associated with love magic that can
be used for sources of seeds, roots, pits, bulbs, and leaves.

♦ Adam-and-eve root
♦ Almond
♦ Apple
♦ Apricot
♦ Blackberry
♦ Carrot
♦ Celery
♦ Cherry
♦ Corn
♦ Daffodil
♦ Date

- Flax
- Hops
- Hyacinth
- Mourning glory
- Orris root
- Peach
- Pear
- Pepper
- Persimmon
- Plum
- Pistachio
- Raspberry
- Rose
- Strawberry
- Tansy
- Wheat

WOOD

Some love spells require a stick of wood or a branch as a talisman or a wand. Here is a list of woods and their correspondences.

- Apple: love
- Birch: sacred to the Goddess or the female principle
- Evergreens: immortality, long life
- Grapevine: joy, intoxication
- Hawthorn: purification, fertility, sacred to Faeries
- Hazel: wisdom, divination, insight
- Holly: Brings power and a winning energy

- Oak: sacred to the God or the male principle
- Rowan or ash: life and protection for the home
- Willow: death, magic

Animals and Birds

Animals and birds have been companions and guides for human beings throughout history. In legend and folklore, animals are often wise counselors, messengers, and examples in matters of the heart. Here are some of the most common animals associated with magic that can be used in love spells and rituals.

Animals

- Black lion
- Boar
- Chinchilla
- Doe
- Dogs: greyhound, poodle, Labrador
- Dolphin
- Dragon
- Goat
- Goldfish
- Gryphon
- Hare
- Hawk
- Horse
- Stag
- Teddy bears

- Toad
- Unicorn
- Water crab
- Whale

Birds

- Bluebird
- Bluejay
- Catbird
- Crane
- Crow
- Magpie
- Mockingbird
- Mourning dove
- Mynah bird
- Parakeet
- Parrot—green or red
- Peach-faced lovebird
- Pheasant
- Raven
- Robin
- Sea gull
- Sparrow
- Swallow
- Swan

FEATHERS

When using feathers as magical tools, try to match the color of the feather with the intention of your spell.

- Red: Great fortune in love and passion.
- Orange: Promise of great delight.
- Yellow: Beware of an untrue lover.
- Green: Adventuresome love or a Faerie lover.
- Blue: Love will enliven your days.
- Brown: Healthy, hearty love.
- Black: Delay; take your time.
- White: You will see the truth of love or a truth about your lover.
- Gray: Be courageous and patient.
- Gray and black: Be careful about what you wish for; be certain.
- Gray and white: All wishes in love will come true.
- Blue, black, and white: Surprises in love, the unexpected.
- Black and white: You have avoided a bad love affair.

MOONS

Many spells are done in conjunction with particular phases of the moon. The following list catalogues the old folk names for the twelve moons of the calendar and for the thirteenth moon we call the Witches' Moon. By incorporating the significance of each moon into your rituals, we draw on the genetic memories of our ancestors who honored each moon in the seasonal activities of the year.

- January: The Wolf Moon—a time to protect loved ones, family, and clan.
- February: The Chaste Moon—a time for renewal, youth, mending a broken heart, making way for a new love as the signs of winter begin to fade.
- March: The Seed Moon—a time for rebirth, to rejuvenate passion, to plant the seeds of a new love.
- April: The Hare Moon—a time for fertility, growth; a time to honor the Goddess Ostara, patron of springtime.
- May: The Dyad Moon—a time to bond, find a partner, double your love, pair up, share.
- June: The Mead Moon—a time to pick fresh flowers, hay, grass for love talismans.
- July: The Wort Moon—a time to gather herbs (worts) to dry for love spells later on.
- August: The Barley Moon—a time to manifest love, cast spells for what you want, harvest the first fruits.
- September: The Wine Moon—a time to celebrate the grape, the intoxicating qualities of love; a time to toast a relationship.
- October: The Blood Moon—a time to recall the blessings of former loves and prepare for winter loving; a time to renew one's commitment to a lover.
- November: The Snow Moon—a time to honor the Snow Queen, the Frost Giants, and the cold cycle of the earth; a time to provide warmth and coziness for loved ones.
- December: The Oak Moon—a time to strengthen a relationship, to build Yule fires, to give gifts to family and friends.

When a month has two moons, the second full moon is referred to as a Blue Moon. We call it the "Witches' Moon" because it is the thirteenth moon in the year, a kind of "moon out of time" or a moon of extra magic and power. Use the time wisely.

COLORS

If you have a choice of colors for paper, cloth, candles, clothing or other magical tools, select the color corresponding to the intention of the spell. The following colors have other significances, but these are the ones most closely related to love.

- ◆ Red: sexual love, passion
- ◆ Pink: love, friendship
- ◆ Orange: strength
- ◆ White: purity, truth
- ◆ Green: fertility
- ◆ Blue: tranquility, healing
- ◆ Brown: house/home

FABRICS

While any fabric can be used for clothing, altar cloths, love philters, beddings, towels, and the like, here are the ones traditionally associated with love. If possible, get them in green, pink, rose, red, or copper.

- ◆ Cotton
- ◆ Cut velvet
- ◆ Linen
- ◆ Plaid/tartan

♦ Silk
♦ Silk satin
♦ Velvet

Prints: moon, stars, hearts, cupids, arrows, flowers.

APHRODISIACS

Aphrodisiacs are common to all societies. Here is a list of herbs and foods, and some charms that are known to be powerful in attracting love.

Foods:

♦ cherries
♦ apples
♦ asparagus
♦ figs
♦ chick-peas
♦ almonds
♦ honey
♦ barley
♦ bamboo shoots
♦ capers

Herbs and seasonings:

♦ rosemary
♦ violet

- coriander
- cardamon
- caraway
- tumeric
- cinnamon
- marjoram
- Damiana liqueur
- basil
- ginger
- paprika
- peppercorns
- verbena

Charms to wear:

- dragon's blood
- lock of a lover's hair
- dove feathers
- cardinal feathers
- roses

Appendix A:
Celtic Gods and Goddesses

HERE is a partial list of the Celtic Gods, Goddesses, Faerie Kings, and Faerie Queens who are powerful nature deities to invoke in love magic. These old names are difficult to pronounce, but use your instincts here as you would with any ancient, magical language.

Gods

- *Aengus mac Ōg:* a God of the Tuatha Dē Danaan. He can bestow youth and beauty on your love life.
- *Bran:* a Celtic Warrior God. Use an apple branch to represent his power, and he will help you win a love.
- *Cuchulainn:* Son of Lug. He can protect you and your lover. Use the number seven for calling on him.
- *The Dagda:* Chief God of the Tuatha Dē Danaan. Call upon him to revive love, or to help you find another land for love magic.

- *Far Darrig:* a Fairy God of the Red Cloak. He can help you escape from a dangerous situation.

- *Fin Bheara:* an Irish God of the Underworld. He can help with divination and attraction magic.

- *Fir Chlis:* a Faerie King known as the Merry Dancer. His magic color is red, which represents Faerie blood. Invoke him with these enigmatic words: "Going up with music on cold starry nights to feast with the Queen of Gay Northern Lights."

- *Green Man:* a divine King of the May. He is the deity of the creative powers in nature who can help bring love back into your life.

- *Gwydion:* a Welsh bard. Call upon him to obtain beauty.

- *Gwyn ap Nudd:* King of the Underworld. He can protect your love.

- *Lug:* called the "Many Skilled." He can be invoked for all love magic.

- *Manannan:* Irish Sea God. He can keep love alive and bring you many new lovers.

- *Merlin:* a Godlike Witch. Call upon him for moon or star magic.

- *Midhir:* a king of the Tuatha Dē Danaan. Call him to find a lover. In the form of a swan, he will help you let go of a lover.

- *Oberon:* Scottish Faerie King. His great magic is very powerful for mortals' love spells.

- *Oisin:* Son of a Deer Goddess. He can help you find an animal totem or familiar to use in love magic.

- *Ogma:* King of the Bards. He can help you find the right words for spells.

♦ *Taliesin:* a Bard. He can help you shapeshift or find the right words to say to a lover.

Goddesses

♦ *Áine:* Celtic Moon Goddess. She brings good luck. Call her on the full moon. Use her image as a swan to bring you love.

♦ *Aisling:* a Faerie Goddess. She brings dreams into reality and reality into dreams.

♦ *Arianrod:* Goddess of the Silver Wheel. Invoke her in star magic and astrological practices. Use the metal silver in her rites.

♦ *Blodewedd:* a Goddess made of flowers. She is natural beauty and will help you realize your own natural beauty. She will help you decide between two lovers.

♦ *Ceasa:* a Highland Mermaid. She embodies the wisdom of the sacred salmon. She grants three wishes. Use them wisely.

♦ *Cerridwen:* the great Mother Goddess. As Mother of all Magic, she sends the other deities and Faeries to enrich your love magic.

♦ *Brigit:* Goddess of Home and Hearth. She brings a lover home again.

♦ *Dôn:* (or Dana, or Irish Star Mother Goddess) a Star Goddess who rules many tribes. Call her upon a star and she will search far and wide to find a love for you.

- *Epona:* Celtic Horse Goddess. She rides on moonlight to bring your message of love to your lover.

- *Etain:* Irish Goddess of the Sidh. Use a chalice or simple goblet to drink to her a libation, asking that she will birth in you the spirit of love.

- *Ethlinn:* the Goddess Lover of Kian. Ask her for help in easing the pain of a broken heart.

- *Morgain:* Goddess of Witches. Her powers are many and she will help all, especially women, to realize their own magic. She will help you shapeshift. Use her form as the crow, her black feather as a magical tool.

- *The Morrigan:* a Goddess of the Black Moon, an Elder. She will protect you and give you strength in love battles.

- *Neman:* Irish War Goddess. Call upon her to end arguments with a loved one. She too appears in the shape of a crow.

- *Lady of the Lake:* a water Faerie. Invoke her aid to transport you to a lover. Drink a libation to her with spring-water.

- *Oonach:* a Faerie Queen. Beautiful, radiant with stars and golden hair, she will help you shapeshift to understand your lover better.

- *Rhiannon:* British and Welsh Goddess. She helps when charging a magic bag of stone and herbs for love. Ask her help in brewing love potions.

- *Scathach:* Warrior Goddess. She will help you protect yourself from a threatening or abusive lover and give you strength to begin life over again.

Appendix B:
Sources for Books, Tools, and Magic

Aphrodisia (A Herb Shop)
62 Kent Street
Brooklyn, NY 11222
1-800-221-6989
Mail order and store

Crow Haven Corner (A Witch Shop)
125 Essex Street
Salem, MA 01970
508-745-8763
Mail order and store

Magic Door (Laurie Cabot Products, Potions, and Magic Tools mentioned in book available)

P.O. Box 8349
Salem, MA 01971–8349
508-744-6274
Mail order only